Transitioning to Common Core

Student Lessons

AF732651

Scott Foresman-Addison Wesley

enVisionMATH™

Authors

Randall I. Charles
Professor Emeritus
Department of Mathematics
San Jose State University
San Jose, California

Janet H. Caldwell
Professor of Mathematics
Rowan University
Glassboro, New Jersey

Mary Cavanagh
Executive Director of Center for Practice,
Research, and Innovation in Mathematics
Education (PRIME)
Arizona State University
Mesa, Arizona

Juanita Copley
Professor Emerita, College of Education
University of Houston
Houston, Texas

Warren Crown
Professor Emeritus of Mathematics Education
Graduate School of Education
Rutgers University
New Brunswick, New Jersey

Francis (Skip) Fennell
L. Stanley Bowlsbey Professor of Education
and Graduate and Professional Studies
McDaniel College
Westminster, Maryland

Stuart J. Murphy
Visual Learning Specialist
Boston, Massachusetts

Kay B. Sammons
Coordinator of Elementary Mathematics
Howard County Public Schools
Ellicott City, Maryland

Jane F. Schielack
Professor of Mathematics
Associate Dean for Assessment and
Pre K-12 Education, College of Science
Texas A&M University
College Station, Texas

William Tate
Edward Mallinckrodt Distinguished University
Professor in Arts & Sciences
Washington University
St. Louis, Missouri

Mathematicians

David M. Bressoud
DeWittWallace Professor of Mathematics
Macalester College
St. Paul, Minnesota

Roger Howe
Professor of Mathematics
Yale University
New Haven, Connecticut

Gary Lippman
Professor of Mathematics and Computer Science
California State University East Bay
Hayward, California

PEARSON

Glenview, Illinois • Boston, Massachusetts • Chandler, Arizona • Upper Saddle River, New Jersey

ELL Consultant

Jim Cummins
Professor
The University of Toronto
Toronto, Canada

Common Core State Standards Reviewers

Elizabeth Baker
Mathematics Coordinator
Gilbert Public Schools
Gilbert, Arizona

Amy Barber
K-12 Math Coach
Peninsula School District ESC
Gig Harbor, Washington

Laura Cua
Teacher
Columbus City Schools
Columbus, Ohio

Wafa Deeb-Westervelt
Assistant Superintendent for Curriculum, Instruction, and Professional Development
Freeport Public Schools
Freeport, New York

Lynn Gullette
Title 1 Math Intervention
Mobile County Public Schools
Gilliard Elementary
Mobile, Alabama

Beverly K. Kimes
Director of Mathematics
Birmingham City Schools
Birmingham, Alabama

Kelly O'Rourke
Elementary School Assistant Principal
Clark County School District
Las Vegas, Nevada

Piper L. Riddle
Evidence-Based Learning Specialist
Canyons School District
Sandy, Utah

Debra L. Vitale
Math Coach
Bristol Public Schools
Bristol, Connecticut

Diane T. Wehby
Math Support Teacher
Birmingham City Schools
Birmingham, Alabama

Scott Foresman-Addison Wesley
enVisionMATH™

ISBN-13: 978-0-328-71544-2
ISBN-10: 0-328-71544-1

1 2 3 4 5 6 7 8 9 10 V011 15 14 13 12 11

Common Core Student Lessons

Name ____________________

Lesson 6-5A
Interactive Learning

Adding Multiples of 10

1. ____ + ____ = ____   ____ + ____ = ____

2. ____ + ____ = ____   ____ + ____ = ____

2.NBT.5 Fluently add and subtract within 100 using strategies based on place value, properties of operations, and/or the relationship between addition and subtraction. Also **2.OA.1, 2.NBT.8, 2.NBT.9**

Home Connection Your child used mental math strategies to add multiples of 10.
Home Activity Search your home with your child to find items he or she can count in groups of tens.

Find 40 + 20.

Adding 4 tens to 2 tens is like adding ones. 4 ones plus 2 ones is 6 ones.

4 tens + 2 tens = 6 tens

4 + 2 = 6, so 40 + 20 = 60.

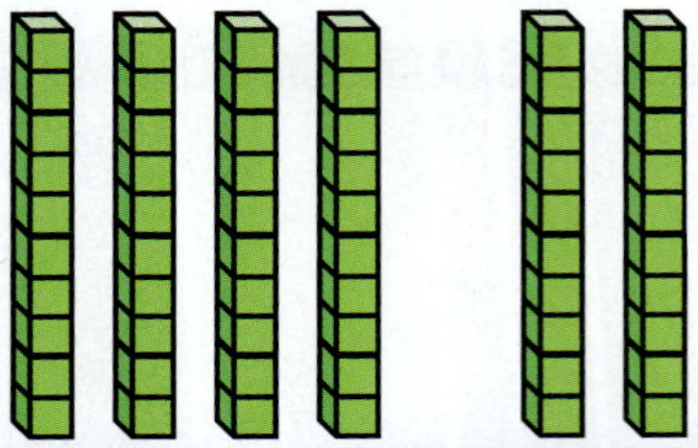

Guided Practice

Add the tens. Use place-value blocks or a hundred chart to help.

1	2	3	4	5	6	7	8	9	10
11	12	13	14	15	16	17	18	19	20
21	22	23	24	25	26	27	28	29	30
31	32	33	34	35	36	37	38	39	40
41	42	43	44	45	46	47	48	49	50
51	52	53	54	55	56	57	58	59	60
61	62	63	64	65	66	67	68	69	70
71	72	73	74	75	76	77	78	79	80
81	82	83	84	85	86	87	88	89	90
91	92	93	94	95	96	97	98	99	100

1. 30 + 50 = 80
2. 40 + 10 = ____
3. 20 + 20 = ____
4. 10 + 30 = ____
5. 50 + 20 = ____
6. 30 + 30 = ____
7. 60 + 20 = ____
8. 70 + 20 = ____

Do you understand? What are two ways you can add 50 + 20?

Another way to add tens is to count on by tens.

Start at 40.
Count on 50, 60.

31	32	33	34	35	36	37	38	39	40
41	42	43	44	45	46	47	48	49	50
51	52	53	54	55	56	57	58	59	60

40 + 20 = 60

Independent Practice

Add the tens. Use place-value blocks or a hundred chart to help.

1	2	3	4	5	6	7	8	9	10
11	12	13	14	15	16	17	18	19	20
21	22	23	24	25	26	27	28	29	30
31	32	33	34	35	36	37	38	39	40
41	42	43	44	45	46	47	48	49	50
51	52	53	54	55	56	57	58	59	60
61	62	63	64	65	66	67	68	69	70
71	72	73	74	75	76	77	78	79	80
81	82	83	84	85	86	87	88	89	90
91	92	93	94	95	96	97	98	99	100

9. 40 + 30 = ____

10. 10 + 30 = ____

11. 20 + 50 = ____

12. 40 + 20 = ____

13. 30 + 60 = ____

14. 50 + 10 = ____

15. 20 + 70 = ____

Algebra Find the missing ten that makes the number sentence true.

16. 60 + ☐ = 80

17. 10 + ☐ = 50

Solve the problems below.

18. The red car and blue car both stand for a number.
Use the clues to figure out each number.

 + 40 = 90

 +  = 80

 = ______

 = ______

19. 3 tens + 50 ones = ______

30	50	70	80
Ⓐ	Ⓑ	Ⓒ	Ⓓ

20. **Journal** Write a number story about 20 monkeys and 10 lions.
Write an addition sentence that tells how many in all.
Use place-value blocks or a hundred chart to help.

____

____

____

____

____ + ____ = ____

DIGITAL eTools www.pearsonsuccessnet.com

Name ____________________

Subtracting Multiples of 10

Interactive Learning Lesson 7-3A

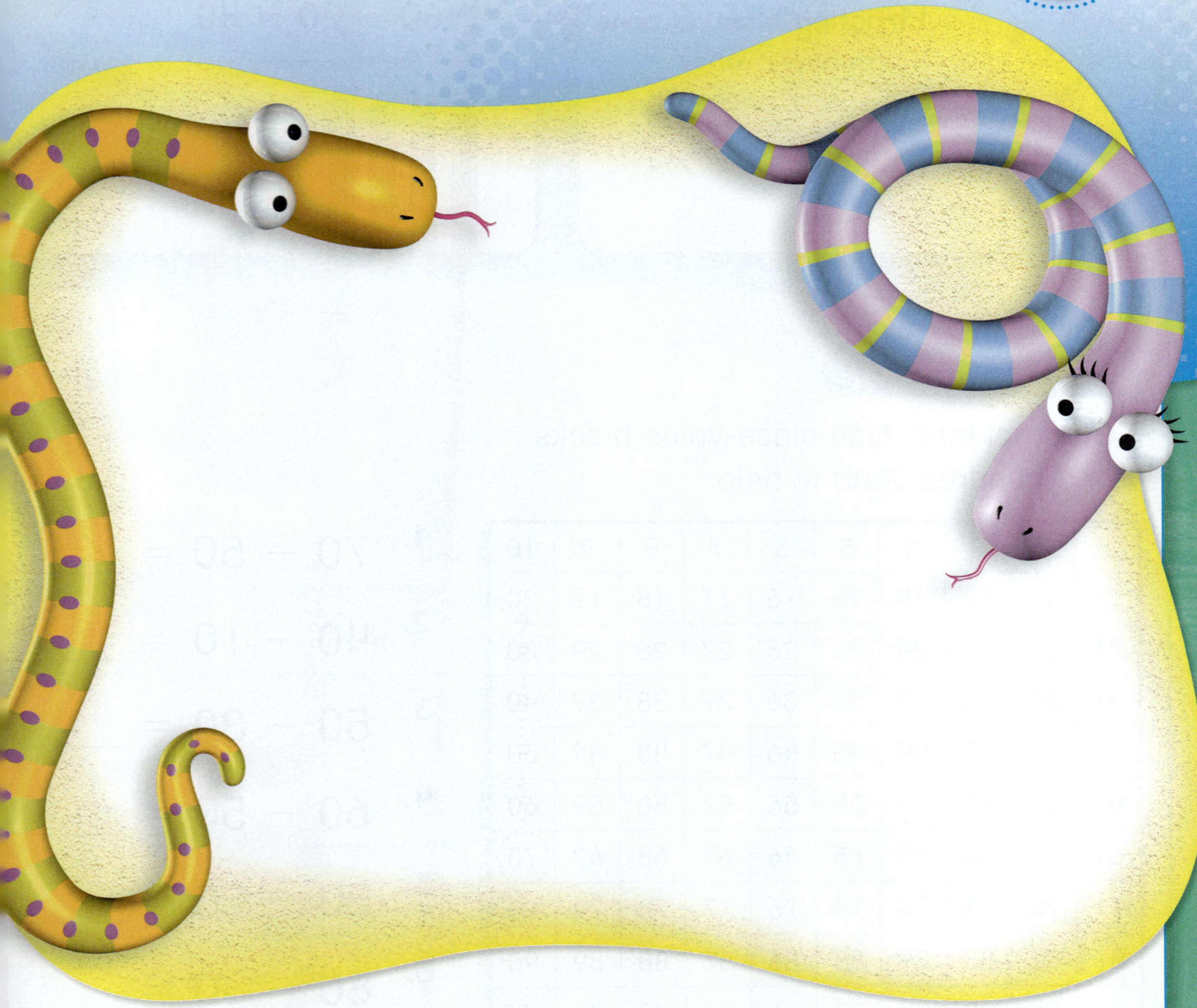

1. ____ − ____ = ____

2. ____ − ____ = ____

2.NBT.5 Fluently add and subtract within 100 using strategies based on place value, properties of operations, and/or the relationship between addition and subtraction. Also **2.OA.1, 2.NBT.8, 2.NBT.9**

Home Connection Your child used mental math strategies to subtract multiples of 10. **Home Activity** Search your home with your child to find items he or she can count in groups of ten.

Find 60 − 20.

Subtracting 2 tens from 6 tens is like subtracting ones. 6 ones minus 2 ones is 4 ones.

6 tens − 2 tens = 4 tens

6 − 2 = 4, so 60 − 20 = 40.

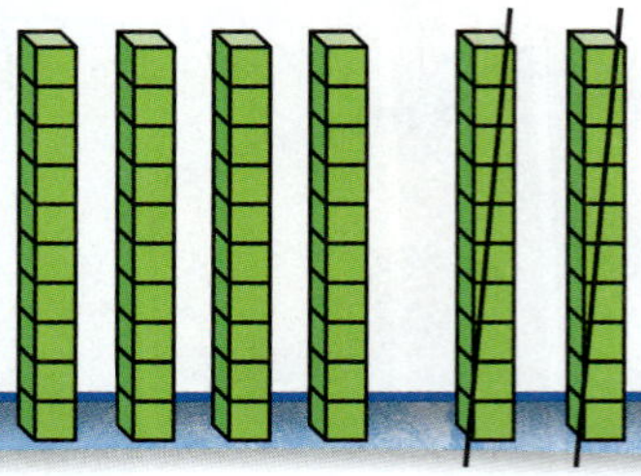

Guided Practice

Subtract tens. Use place-value blocks or a hundred chart to help.

1	2	3	4	5	6	7	8	9	10
11	12	13	14	15	16	17	18	19	20
21	22	23	24	25	26	27	28	29	30
31	32	33	34	35	36	37	38	39	40
41	42	43	44	45	46	47	48	49	50
51	52	53	54	55	56	57	58	59	60
61	62	63	64	65	66	67	68	69	70
71	72	73	74	75	76	77	78	79	80
81	82	83	84	85	86	87	88	89	90
91	92	93	94	95	96	97	98	99	100

1. 70 − 50 = 20
2. 40 − 10 = ____
3. 50 − 30 = ____
4. 60 − 50 = ____
5. 30 − 20 = ____
6. 80 − 30 = ____
7. 90 − 60 = ____
8. 80 − 70 = ____

Do you understand? What are two ways you can subtract 70 − 50?

Another way to subtract tens is to count back by tens.

31	32	33	34	35	36	37	38	39	40
41	42	43	44	45	46	47	48	49	50
51	52	53	54	55	56	57	58	59	60

60 − 20 = 40

Independent Practice

Subtract tens. Use place-value blocks or a hundred chart to help.

1	2	3	4	5	6	7	8	9	10
11	12	13	14	15	16	17	18	19	20
21	22	23	24	25	26	27	28	29	30
31	32	33	34	35	36	37	38	39	40
41	42	43	44	45	46	47	48	49	50
51	52	53	54	55	56	57	58	59	60
61	62	63	64	65	66	67	68	69	70
71	72	73	74	75	76	77	78	79	80
81	82	83	84	85	86	87	88	89	90
91	92	93	94	95	96	97	98	99	100

9. 40 − 30 = ____

10. 60 − 30 = ____

11. 50 − 20 = ____

12. 30 − 10 = ____

13. 80 − 50 = ____

14. 70 − 10 = ____

15. 90 − 80 = ____

Algebra Find the missing ten that makes the number sentence true.

16. 60 − ☐ = 40

17. 80 − ☐ = 40

Problem Solving

MATHEMATICAL PRACTICES

Solve the problems below.

18. The pet store has three kinds of toys. Use the clues to find out how many of each toy.

Octo

Star

Crabby

Clues: They have 30 Crabbys.
They have 20 less Stars than Crabbys.
They have 10 more Octos than Stars.

How many Stars are there? _____

How many Octos are there? _____

19. 5 tens − 20 ones = _____

Ⓐ 30	Ⓑ 50	Ⓒ 70	Ⓓ 80

20. **Journal** Write a number story about a group of 50 snakes. Write a subtraction sentence that tells how many were left over after 20 snakes moved away. Use place-value blocks or a hundred chart to help.

____

____

____

_____ − _____ = _____

DIGITAL eTools www.pearsonsuccessnet.com

Name ____________________

Adding on a Number Line

Interactive Learning
Lesson 8-6A

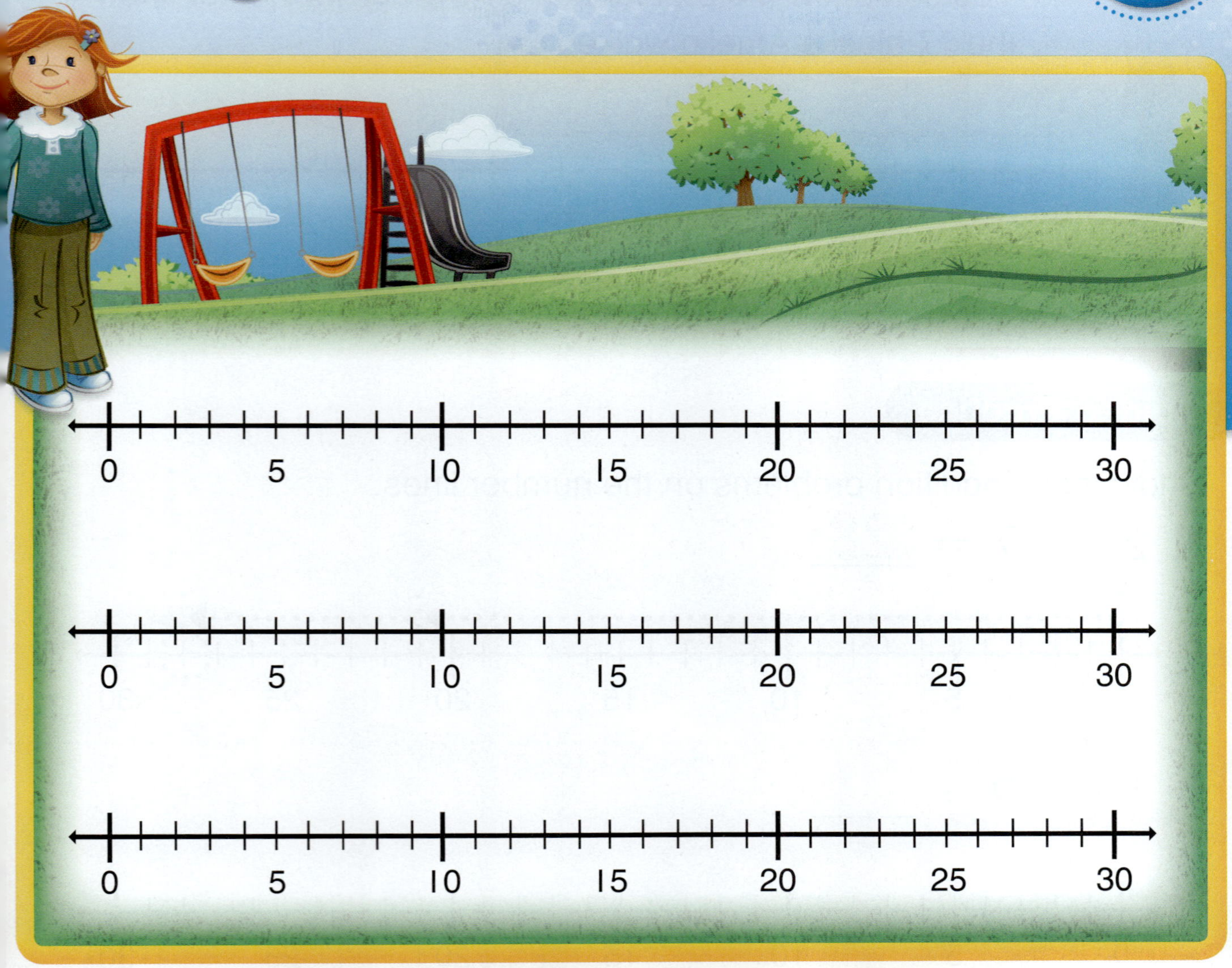

1. ____ + ____ = ____

2. ____ + ____ = ____

3. ____ + ____ = ____

2.MD.6 Represent whole numbers as lengths from 0 on a number line diagram with equally spaced points corresponding to the numbers 0, 1, 2, ..., and represent whole-number sums and differences within 100 on a number line diagram. Also **2.NBT.5, 2.NBT.6, 2.NBT.9**

Home Connection Your child used a number line to add two-digit numbers.
Home Activity Create a number line at home and use it to count the number of steps from one room or place to the next. Then count the number of steps from the last place to a different room or place and add that number to the original number of steps using the number line.

Amelia walked 17 blocks before dinner. She walked 8 blocks after dinner. How many blocks did she walk in all?

You can show the problem on a **number line**. First show the 17 blocks Amelia walked.

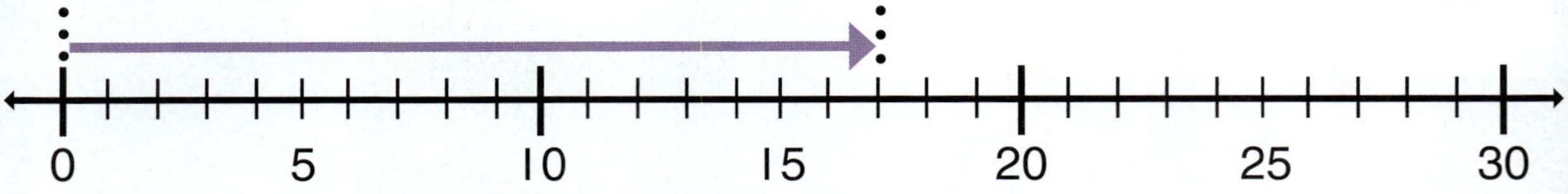

Guided Practice

Show these addition problems on the number lines.

1. $21 + 7 =$ 28

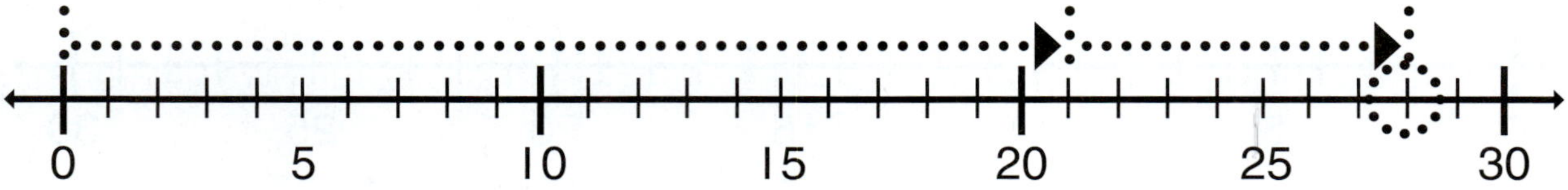

2. $14 + 9 =$ ____

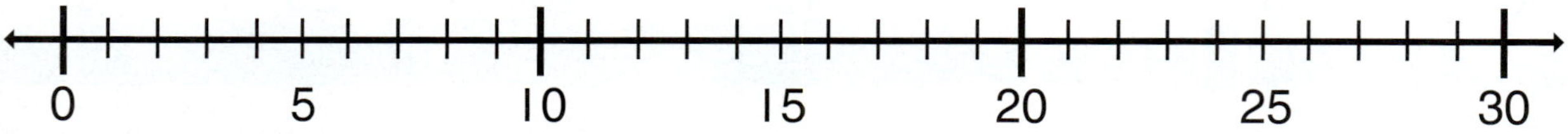

What addition problem does this number line show?

3. ____ + ____ = ____

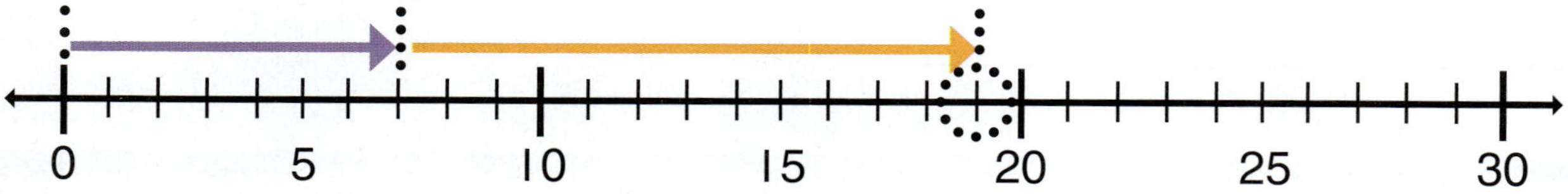

Do you understand? Explain how to show $7 + 11$ on the number line.

Then show the 8 blocks she walked after dinner.
Amelia walked 25 blocks in all.

17 + 8 = 25

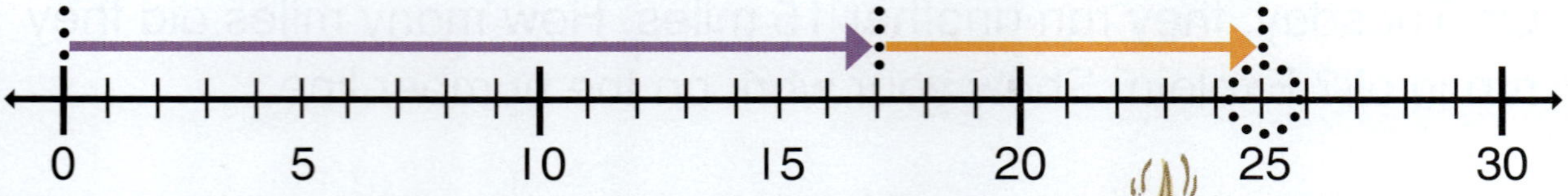

Word Bank
number line

Independent Practice

Show this addition problem on the number line.

4. 16 + 5 = ____

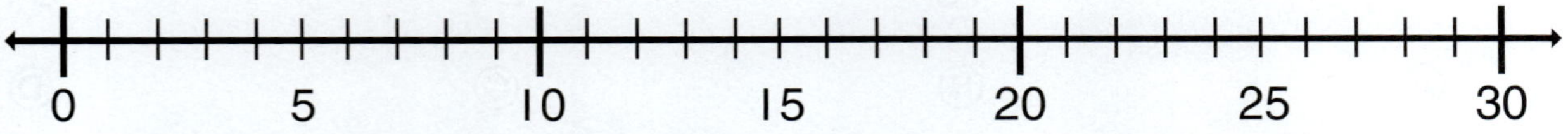

What addition problems do these number lines show?

5. ____ + ____ = ____

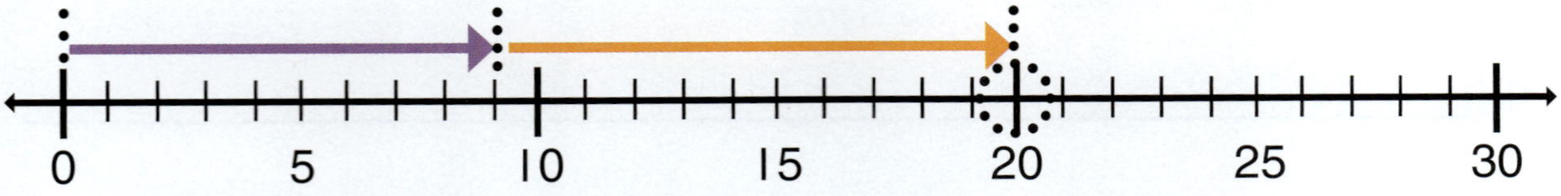

6. ____ + ____ = ____

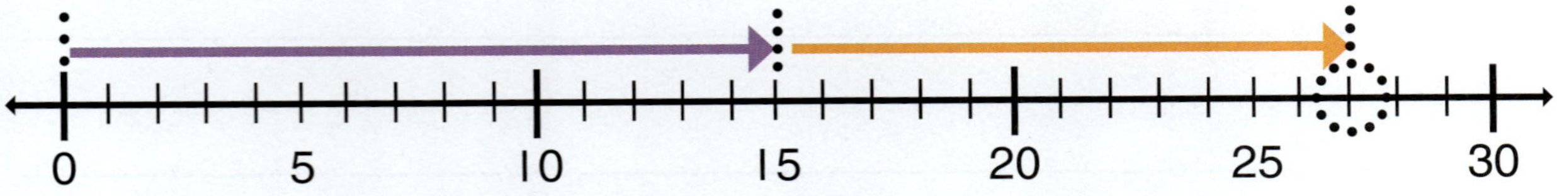

Reasoning

7. You show an addition problem on a number line. Will the sum always be farther along the number line than the first number you show?

Problem Solving

MATHEMATICAL PRACTICES

Solve the problems below.

8. The runners on Samantha's track team ran 15 miles on Monday. On Tuesday, they ran another 15 miles. How many miles did they run in all? Explain. Show your work on the number line.

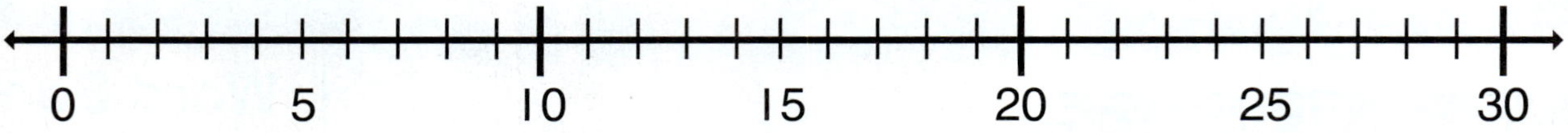

9. Lakisha draws 15 blue horses. Liam draws 9 green horses. How many horses did they draw in all?

9	15	24	34
Ⓐ	Ⓑ	Ⓒ	Ⓓ

10. **Journal** Describe how to solve $9 + 13$ using a number line.

Name ______________________________

Interactive Learning
Lesson 9-6A

Subtracting on a Number Line

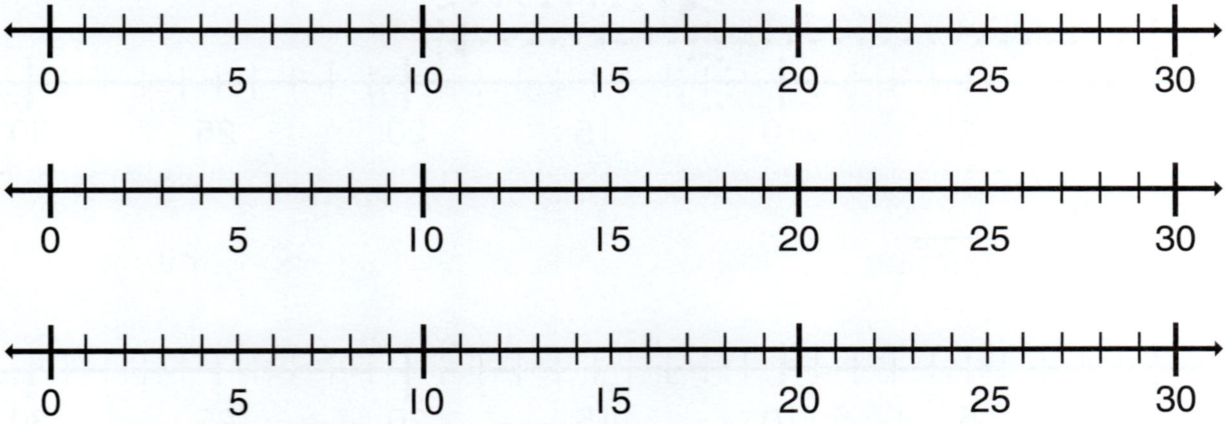

1. _____ − _____ = _____

2. _____ − _____ = _____

3. _____ − _____ = _____

2.MD.6 Represent whole numbers as lengths from 0 on a number line diagram with equally spaced points corresponding to the numbers 0, 1, 2, ..., and represent whole-number sums and differences within 100 on a number line diagram. Also **2.NBT.5, 2.NBT.9, 2.NBT.6**

Home Connection Your child used a number line to subtract two-digit numbers.
Home Activity Create a number line at home and use it to count the number of steps from one room or place to the next. Then count the number of steps to a different room or place and subtract that from the original number using the number line.

Grant had 27 cents to spend on a snack. He bought an apple for 15 cents. How much did he have left?

You can show this problem on a number line.
First show the 27 cents that Grant had.

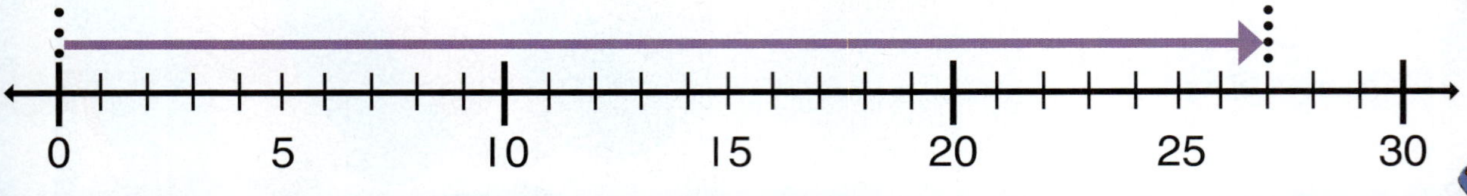

Guided Practice

Show these subtraction problems on the number lines.

1. 19 − 7 = 12

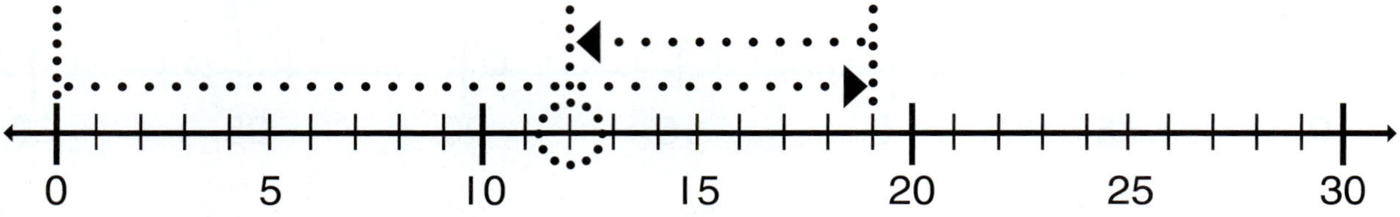

2. 28 − 14 = ______

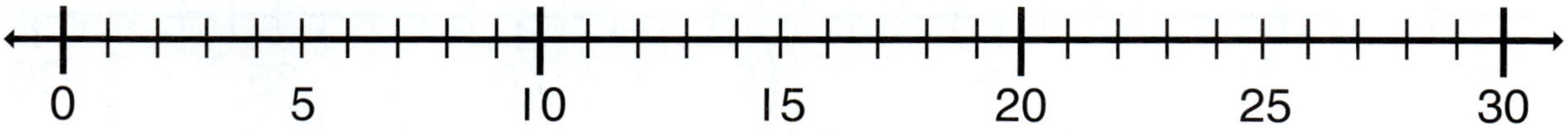

What subtraction problem does this number line show?

3. ______ − ______ = ______

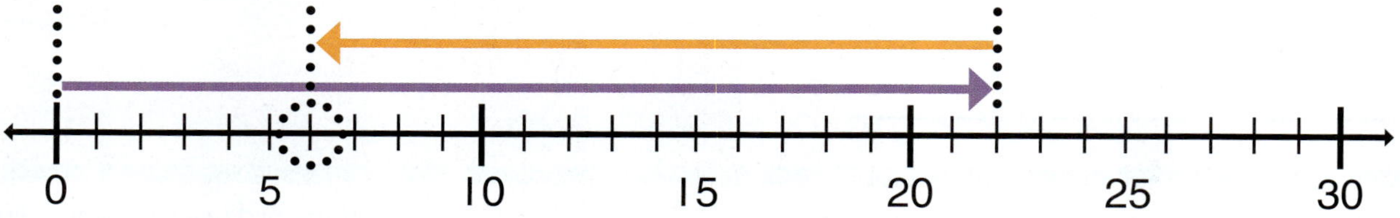

Do you understand? Explain how to show 25 − 13 on a number line.

Then show the 15 cents he spent. That line goes the other way because it is being subtracted.
He has 12 cents left.

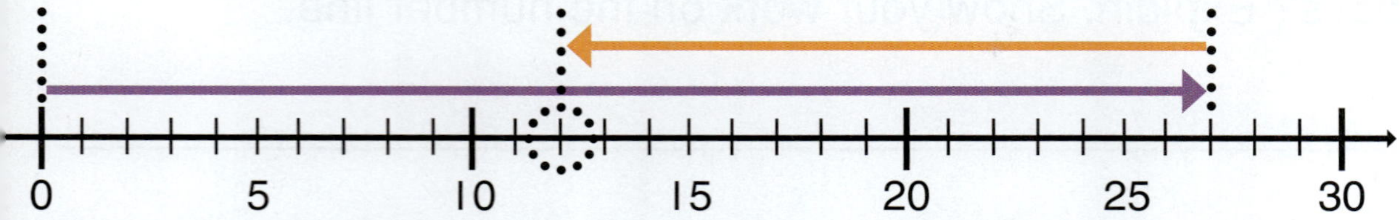

Independent Practice

Show this subtraction problem on a number line.

4. 26 − 5 = _____

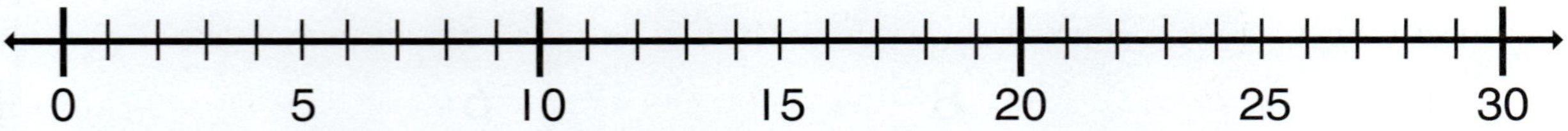

What subtraction problems do these number lines show?

5. _____ − _____ = _____

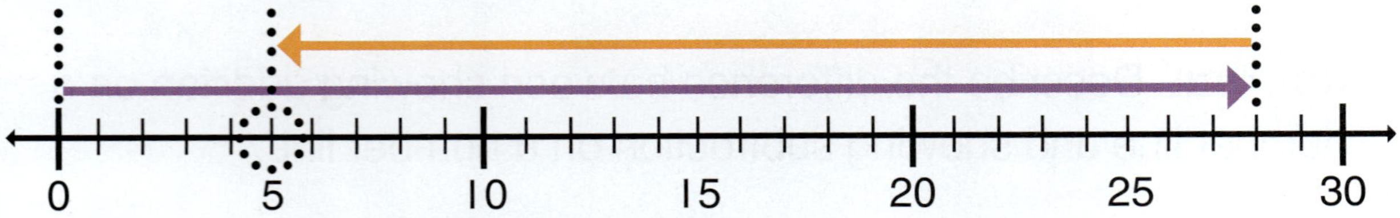

6. _____ − _____ = _____

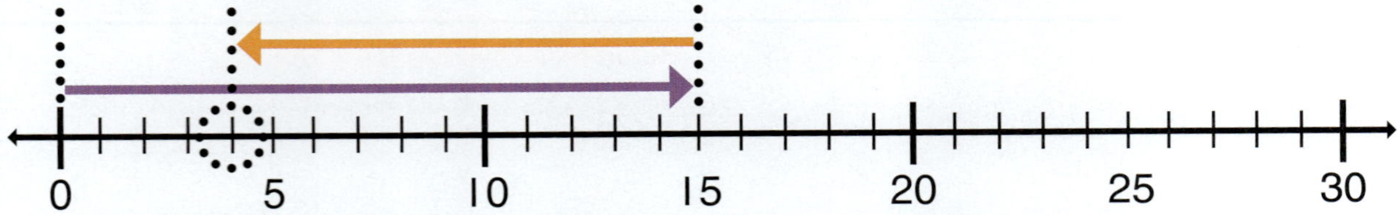

Reasoning How do you show 12 − 0 on a number line?

Problem Solving

MATHEMATICAL PRACTICES

Solve the problems below.

7. All 29 children in Grant's class went to the school fair. 16 of them are girls. How many of the remaining students are boys? Explain. Show your work on the number line.

____

____

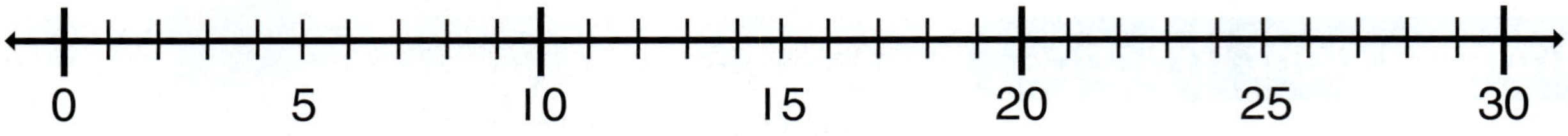

8. 23 − 17 = _____

17	8	6	4
Ⓐ	Ⓑ	Ⓒ	Ⓓ

9. **Journal** Describe the difference between showing addition on a number line and showing subtraction on a number line.

____

____

____

DIGITAL eTools www.pearsonsuccessnet.com

Name ____________________

Polygons and Angles

Interactive Learning
Lesson 11-3A

1. 3 sides, 3 angles, and 3 vertices

____

2. 4 sides, 4 angles, and 4 vertices

____

3. 5 sides, 5 angles, and 5 vertices

____

4. 6 sides, 6 angles, and 6 vertices

____

2.G.1 Recognize and draw shapes having specified attributes, such as a given number of angles or a given number of equal faces. Identify triangles, quadrilaterals, pentagons, hexagons, and cubes.

Home Connection Your child identified various polygons and their attributes.
Home Activity Walk around your home and look for items that are shaped like triangles, quadrilaterals, pentagons, or hexagons. Ask your child to tell you how many sides, vertices, and angles each shape has.

Triangles	Not Triangles	**Quadrilaterals**	Not Quadrilaterals
	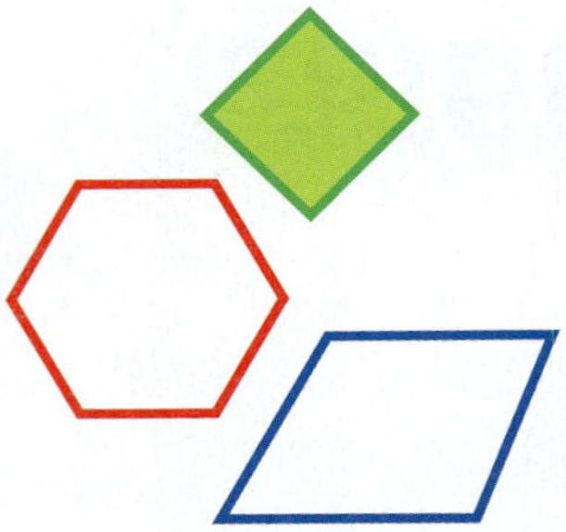	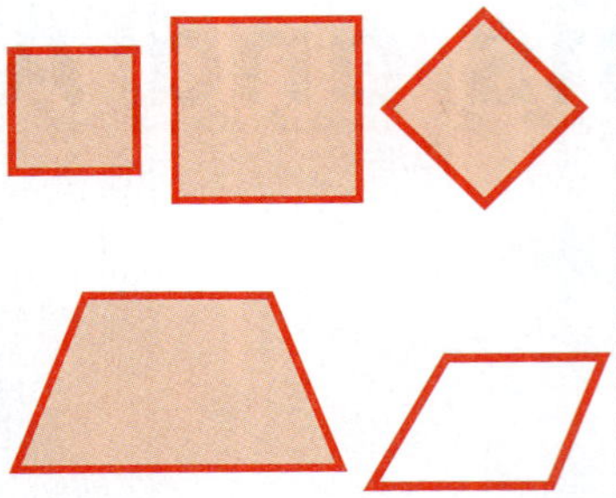	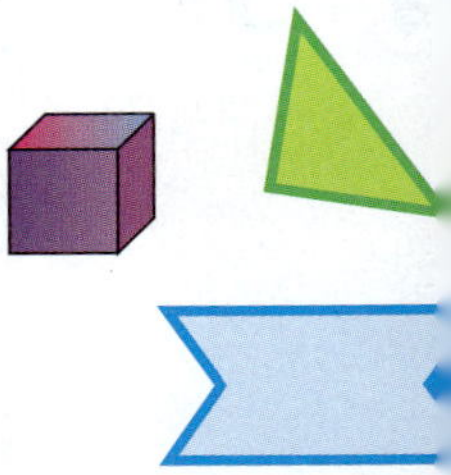
3 **sides**, 3 vertices, 3 **angles**		4 sides, 4 vertices, 4 angles	

Guided Practice

1. Match each shape to its correct name.

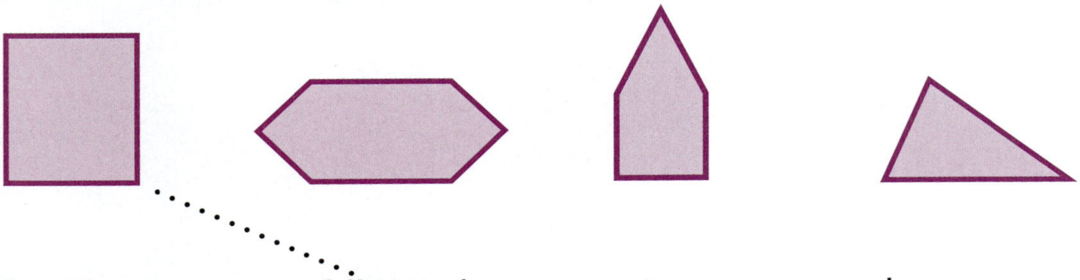

triangle   quadrilateral   pentagon   hexagon

Name the shape. Tell how many sides, angles, and vertices.

2.

______ sides

______ vertices

______ angles

Shape: ________________

3.

______ sides

______ vertices

______ angles

Shape: ________________

Do you understand? How do sides, angles, and vertices help you name a polygon?

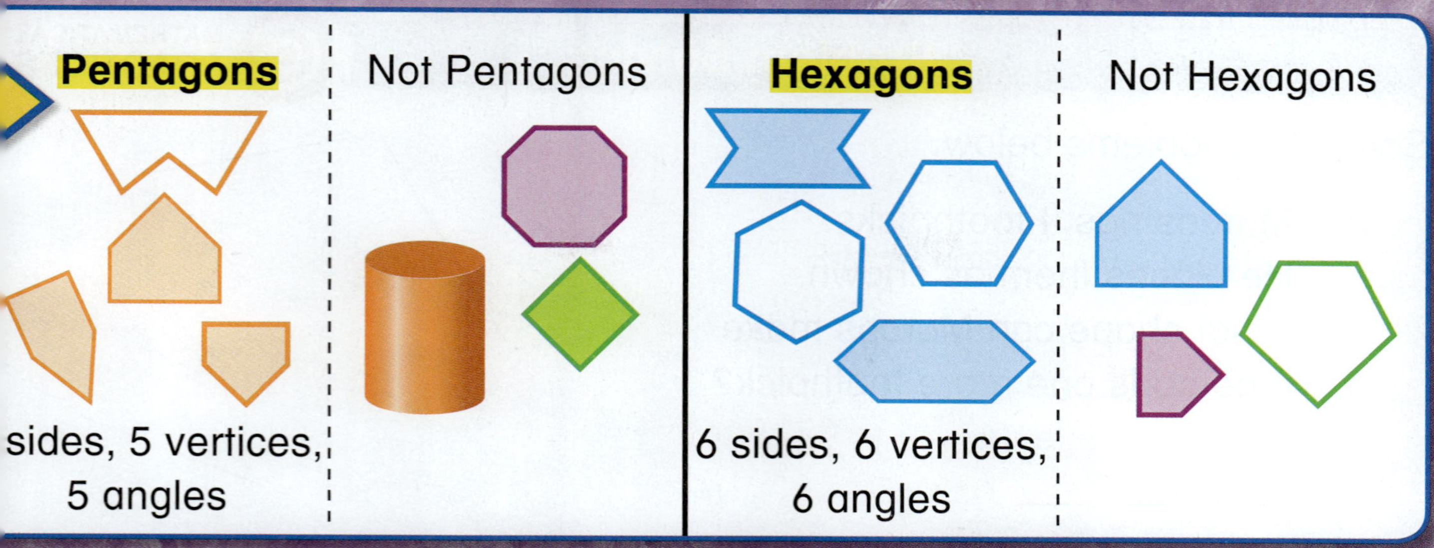

Independent Practice

Word Bank
side
angle
quadrilateral
pentagon
hexagon

4. Match each shape to its correct name.

triangle quadrilateral pentagon hexagon

Draw the shape. Tell how many sides, angles, and vertices.

5. Quadrilateral

_____ sides

_____ vertices

_____ angles

6. Hexagon

_____ sides

_____ vertices

_____ angles

Geometry

7. How many vertices does a shape with 6 angles have?

_____

Problem Solving

MATHEMATICAL PRACTICES

Solve the problems below.

8. Marcos has 4 toothpicks.
He places them as shown.
What shape can Marcos make
if he adds one more toothpick?

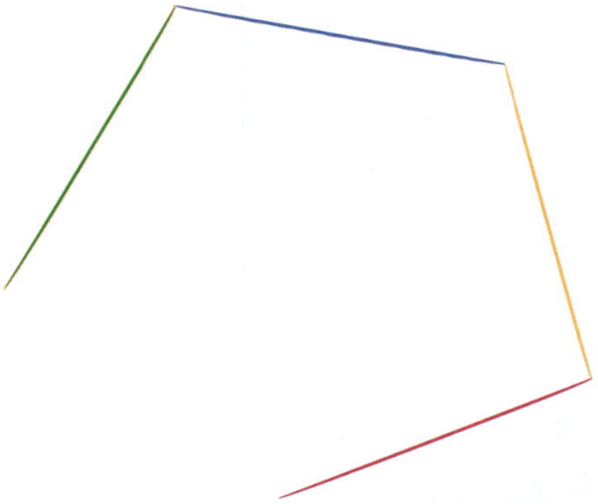

____

9. Which is the name of this polygon?

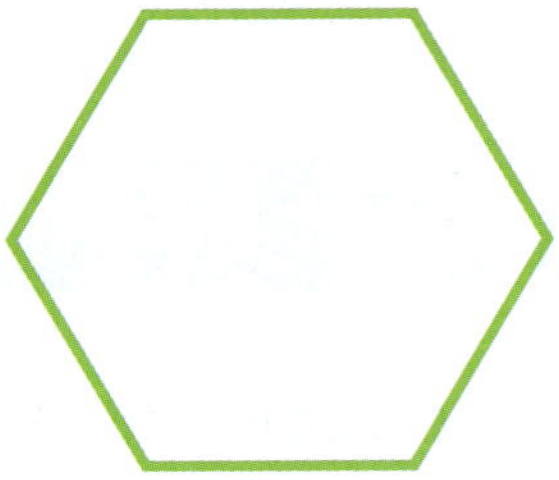

square	quadrilateral	pentagon	hexagon
Ⓐ	Ⓑ	Ⓒ	Ⓓ

10. **Journal** Randall said that a square is a quadrilateral. Susan said that a square is a square, so it is not a quadrilateral. Who is right? Why?

____

____

____

____

____

____

DIGITAL eTools www.pearsonsuccessnet.com

Name ____

Dividing Rectangles into Equal Squares

Columns

Rows

____ squares

Rows: ____ + ____ + ____ + ____ = ____ squares

Columns: ____ + ____ + ____ + ____ = ____ squares

2.G.2 Partition a rectangle into rows and columns of same-size squares and count to find the total number of them.

Home Connection Your child divided rectangles into equal squares.
Home Activity In your home or the grocery store, notice the tiles on the floor. Ask your child to mark off a rectangle and count how many squares make up that rectangle.

How many squares can cover this rectangle?

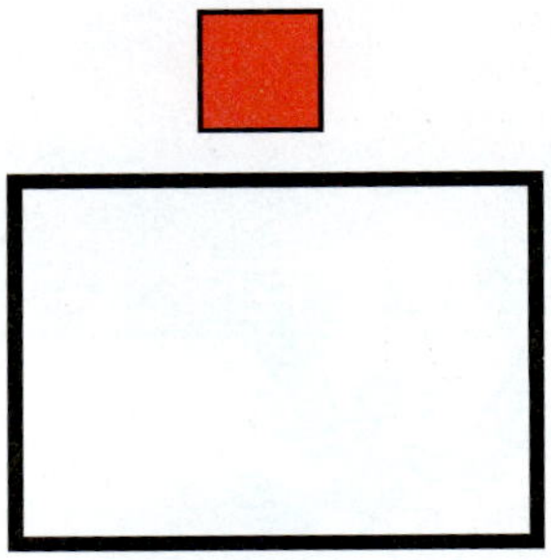

Begin like this:

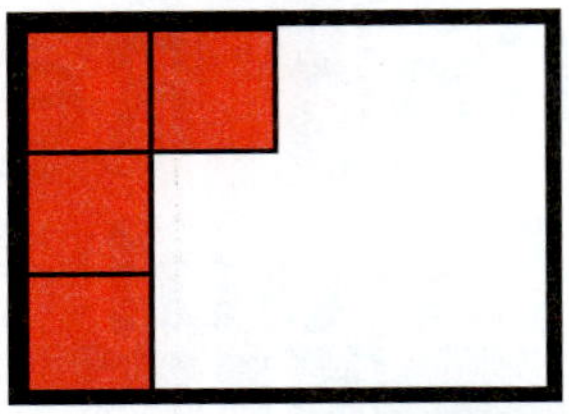

NOT like this:

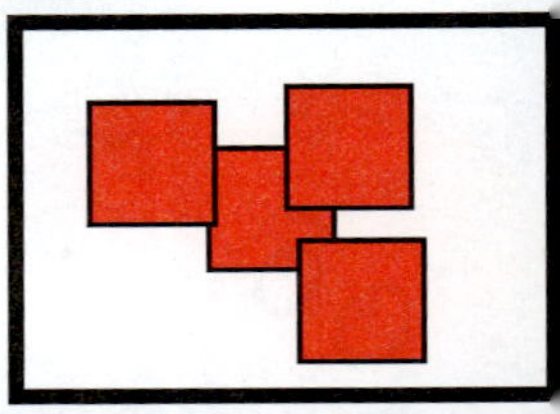

Guided Practice

1. Use square tiles to cover the rectangle. Trace the tiles to show your work.

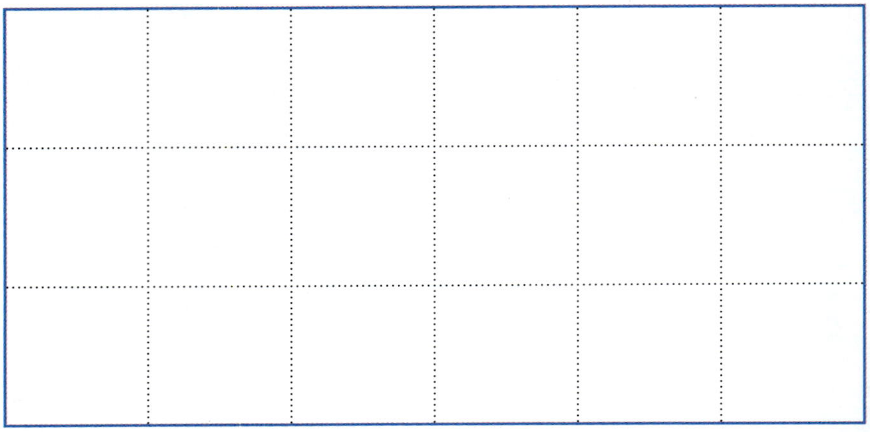

2. How many squares cover the rectangle?

Count by rows: ____ + ____ + ____ = ____

Count by columns: ____ + ____ + ____ + ____ + ____ + ____ = ____

Do you understand? How can you use tiles to divide a rectangle into equal squares?

Count the squares by **rows**.

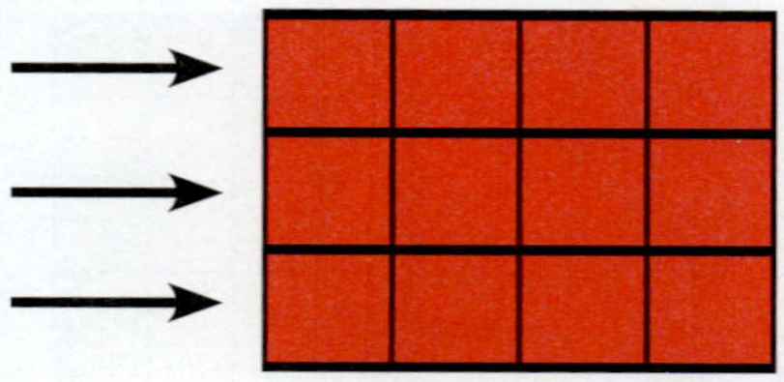

$4 + 4 + 4 = 12$

Count the squares by **columns**.

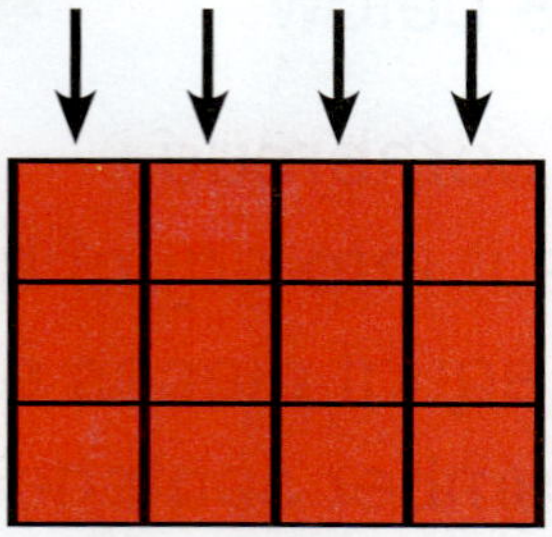

$3 + 3 + 3 + 3 = 12$

Independent Practice

Word Bank
row column

3. Use square tiles to cover the rectangle. Trace the tiles to show your work.

4. How many squares cover the rectangle?

Count by rows: ____ + ____ + ____ + ____ = ____

Count by columns: ____ + ____ + ____ + ____ + ____ = ____

Reasoning

5. Draw a rectangle that is divided into equal squares.

Solve the problems below.

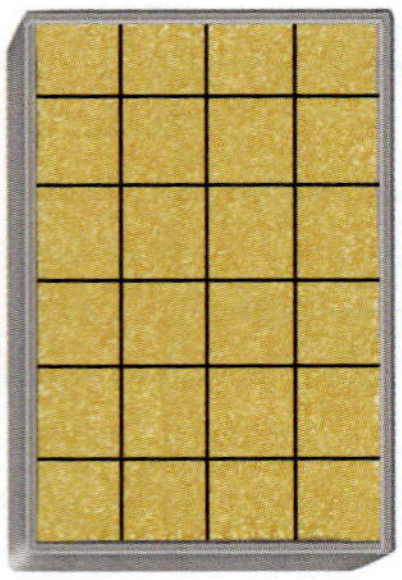

6. Lisa bakes cornbread.
She divides it into equal square pieces.
How many equal pieces are there?
Write two number sentences to show your work.

Rows: ____ + ____ + ____ + ____ + ____ + ____ = ____

Columns: ____ + ____ + ____ + ____ = ____

7. Chan divided a rectangle into equal squares.
He counted the squares by rows.
He also counted by columns.
What could the rectangle look like?

$5 + 5 = 10$

$2 + 2 + 2 + 2 + 2 = 10$

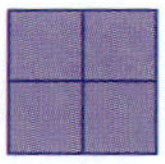

Ⓐ

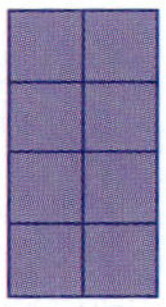

Ⓑ

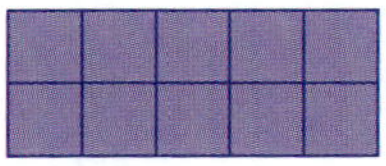

Ⓒ

Ⓓ

8. Journal Draw a square. Then divide it into equal squares. What do you notice about the number of rows and columns?

____

____

____

____

DIGITAL eTools www.pearsonsuccessnet.com

Name ______________________________

Interactive Learning
Lesson 13-4A

Inches

about 1 inch	about 6 inches	about 12 inches
1. ______________	**2.** ______________	**3.** ______________

2.MD.1 Measure the length of an object by selecting and using appropriate tools such as rulers, yardsticks, meter sticks, and measuring tapes. Also **2.MD.3**

Home Connection Your child identified classroom objects that measure about 1 inch, about 6 inches, and about 12 inches long.
Home Activity Ask your child to find items at home that are about 1 inch, about 6 inches, and about 12 inches long.

You can measure the **length**, **width**, and **height** of an object in **inches (in.)**.

To measure to the **nearest inch**, look for the halfway mark.

Guided Practice

Estimate the height or length of each object.
Then use a ruler to measure.

	Estimate	Measure
1. 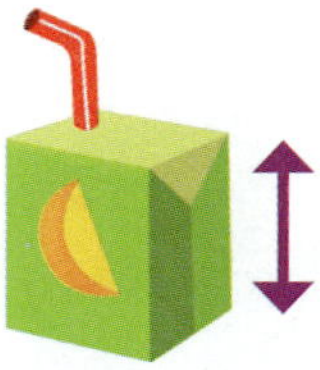 height of a juice box	About 6 inches	About 4 inches
2. 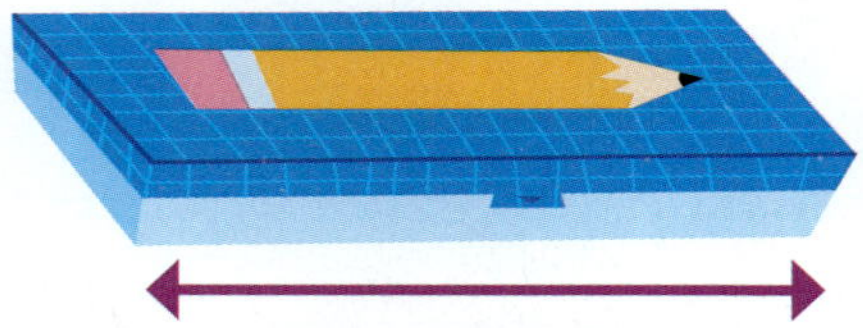 length of a pencil case	About _____ inches	About _____ inches
3.  length of a book bag	About _____ inches	About _____ inches

Do you understand? What classroom objects are about 12 inches long?

If the object is longer than the halfway mark, use the greater number.

If the object is shorter than the halfway mark, use the smaller number.

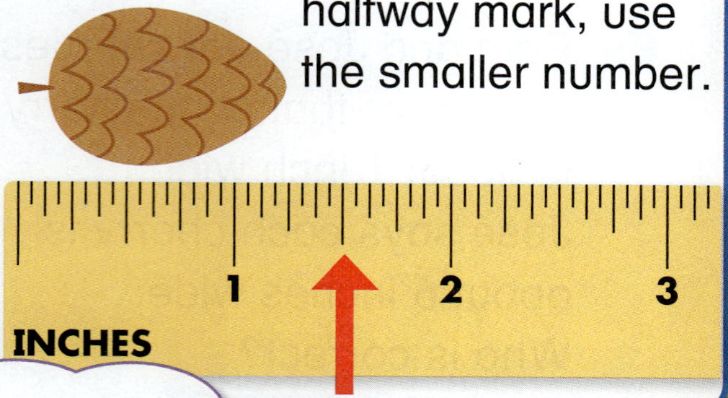

Word Bank
length
width
height
inch (in.)
nearest inch

Independent Practice

Estimate the height or length of each object. Then use a ruler to measure.

	Estimate	Measure
4. 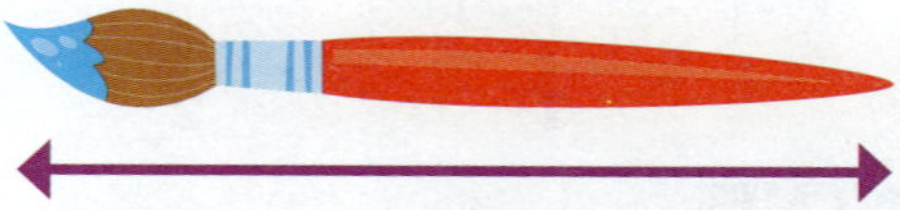 length of a paintbrush	About _____ inches	About _____ inches
5.  height of a cup	About _____ inches	About _____ inches
6.  length of a crayon box	About _____ inches	About _____ inches

Estimation

7. About how many inches long is your arm from your elbow to your wrist?

About _____ inches

Problem Solving

MATHEMATICAL PRACTICES

Solve the problems below.

8. Pam and José eat cherries. Pam says that each cherry is about 1 inch wide. José says each cherry is about 6 inches wide. Who is correct?

____

9. Yona bought a stamp. She measured it with a ruler. Which shows about how long Yona's stamp is?

4 inches	3 inches	2 inches	1 inch
Ⓐ	Ⓑ	Ⓒ	Ⓓ

10. **Journal** Find an object in the classroom that measures about 6 inches. Draw the object. Write two sentences to describe it.

____

____

____

DIGITAL eTools www.pearsonsuccessnet.com

Name ____________________

Centimeters

Interactive Learning
Lesson 13-5A

about 1 centimeter	about 10 centimeters	about 100 centimeters
1. ____________	**2.** ____________	**3.** ____________

2.MD.1 Measure the length of an object by selecting and using appropriate tools such as rulers, yardsticks, meter sticks, and measuring tapes. Also 2.MD.3

Home Connection Your child identified classroom objects that measure about 1 centimeter, about 10 centimeters, and about 100 centimeters.
Home Activity Ask your child to find items at home that measure about 1 centimeter, about 10 centimeters, and about 100 centimeters. If possible, use a ruler to measure each object.

You can measure the length of an object in **centimeters (cm)**.

To measure to the **nearest centimeter**, look for the halfway mark.

Guided Practice

Estimate the width, height, or length of each object. Then use a ruler to measure.

1. 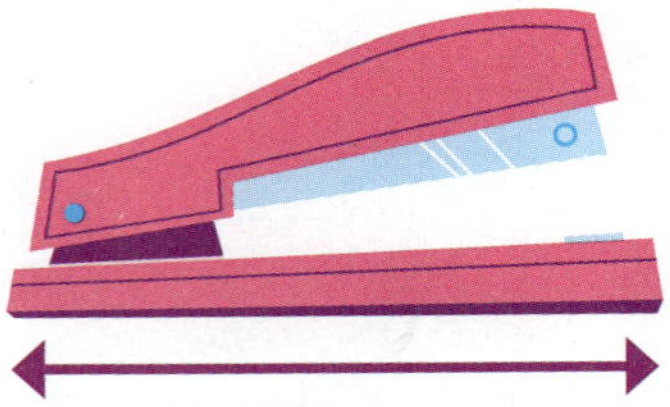
length of a stapler

2. 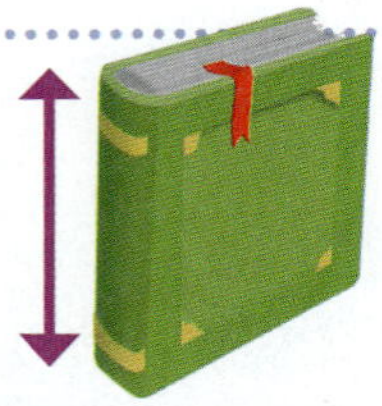
height of a book

3. 
width of a shoelace

	Estimate	Measure
1.	About 15 centimeters	About 18 centimeters
2.	About _____ centimeters	About _____ centimeters
3.	About _____ centimeters	About _____ centimeters

Do you understand? Is the length of a paper clip about 3 centimeters? Explain how you know.

If the object is longer than the halfway mark, use the greater number.

If the object is shorter than the halfway mark, use the smaller number.

Word Bank
centimeter (cm)
nearest centimeter

Independent Practice

Estimate the width, height, or length of each object. Then use a ruler to measure.

		Estimate	Measure
4.	 width of a chair	About _____ centimeters	About _____ centimeters
5.	 length of a pencil	About _____ centimeters	About _____ centimeters
6.	 height of scissors	About _____ centimeters	About _____ centimeters

Estimation

7. Josh estimated that the length of his reading book is about 6 centimeters. Is his estimation reasonable? Explain.

Problem Solving

MATHEMATICAL PRACTICES

Solve the problems below.

8. Paul says a toothbrush is about 15 centimeters long. Sarah says it is about 150 centimeters long. Who is correct, Paul or Sarah?

____

9. Mary wants to know about how long her eraser is to the nearest centimeter.

Which shows about how long Mary's eraser is?

2 centimeters	3 centimeters	4 centimeters	5 centimeters
Ⓐ	Ⓑ	Ⓒ	Ⓓ

10. **Journal** Draw an object that is about 5 centimeters long. Write two sentences to describe your object.

____

____

____

DIGITAL eTools www.pearsonsuccessnet.com

Name ______________________________

Measuring Length

Interactive Learning
Lesson 13-6A

1. about _____ cubes long

about _____ paper clips long

2. about _____ cubes long

about _____ paper clips long

3. about _____ cubes long

about _____ paper clips long

4. about _____ cubes long

about _____ paper clips long

2.MD.2 Measure the length of an object twice, using length units of different lengths for the two measurements; describe how the two measurements relate to the size of the unit chosen.

Home Connection Your child used a connecting cube and a paper clip, as well as inches, feet, and yards to measure objects.
Home Activity Have your child use a foot ruler to measure objects. Then ask your child if he or she measured each object with more inches or more feet.

You can use different units to measure objects. Which would you use more of to measure the length of the bookcase? Feet or yards?

Measure the bookcase with feet.

It is about 3 feet long.

Guided Practice

Measure each object using different units.
Circle the unit you need more of to measure each object.

1.

about _____ feet about _____ yards

more feet

more yards

2.

about _____ inches about _____ feet

more inches

more feet

Do you understand? Would it be easier to measure the height of a door in inches or yards? Why?

Independent Practice

Measure each object using different units.
Circle the unit you need fewer of to measure each object.

3.

about _____ inches   about _____ feet

fewer inches

fewer feet

4.

about _____ feet   about _____ yards

fewer feet

fewer yards

Reasonableness

5. About how long is a key?

about 2 yards   about 2 inches   about 2 feet

Measure to solve the problems below.

6. Measure an object in your classroom using two different units.

Object: ________________ about ________________________

about ________________________

Which unit did you use more of? ________________________

7. Which unit would you need fewer of to measure the table?

fewer inches	fewer feet	fewer yards	all the same
Ⓐ	Ⓑ	Ⓒ	Ⓓ

8. **Journal** Shane and Orna want to measure the length of a soccer field in centimeters or meters. Which unit is easier to measure with? Explain.

____

____

____

____

DIGITAL eTools www.pearsonsuccessnet.com

Name ____________________

Adding and Subtracting in Measurement

Interactive Learning Lesson 13-6B

1. ____ ◯ ____ ◯ ____ ◯ ____ = ____

Distance around: ____

2. Object: ____________

____ ◯ ____ ◯ ____ ◯ ____ = ____

Distance around: ____

3. Object: ____________

____ ◯ ____ ◯ ____ ◯ ____ = ____

Distance around: ____

2.MD.5 Use addition and subtraction within 100 to solve word problems involving lengths that are given in the same units, e.g., by using drawings (such as drawings of rulers) and equations with a symbol for the unknown number to represent the problem.

Home Connection Your child used centimeter and inch rulers to measure the lengths of the sides of rectangular objects. Then he or she added to find the distance around the flat surface of each object.

Home Activity Give your child a rectangular object, such as a postcard or envelope, and a ruler. Ask your child to measure the length of each side to the nearest inch or centimeter and find the distance around the flat surface of the object. Repeat for another object.

One side of this book is 9 inches long and the other side of this book is 6 inches long.

What is the distance around the cover of the book?

You can add the lengths of a… four sides to find the distance around the cover.

$9 + 6 + 9 + 6 = ?$
$9 + 6 + 9 + 6 = 30$

The distance around the cover of the book is 30 inches.

Guided Practice

Write a number sentence to help you solve each problem.

1. What is the distance around the baseball card?

$10 + 7 + 10 + 7 = 34$

Distance around: 34 cm

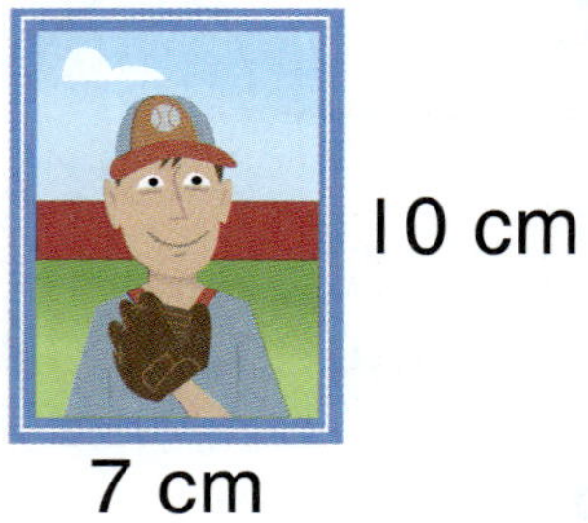

2. What is the distance around the puzzle?

____

Distance around: _____ in.

3. How much longer is the red scarf than the blue scarf?

____

_____ in. longer

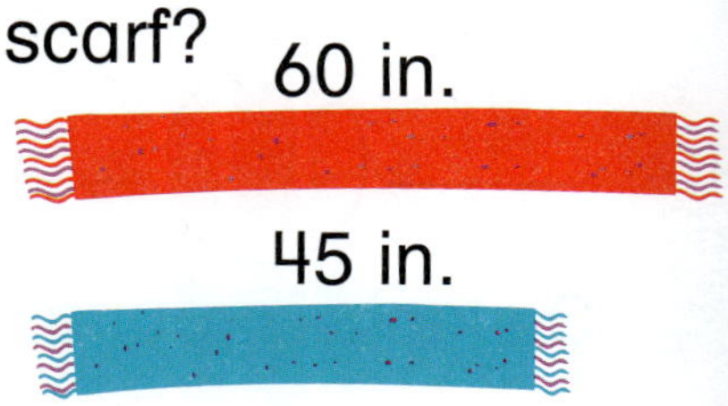

Do you understand? Did you use the same operation to solve Exercises 2 and 3? Explain.

How much longer is the teacher's arm than the child's arm?

You can subtract to compare measurements.

66 − 47 = ?

$$\begin{array}{r} \overset{5}{\cancel{6}}\overset{16}{\cancel{6}} \\ -\,47 \\ \hline 19 \end{array}$$

The teacher's arm is 19 centimeters longer than the child's arm.

Independent Practice

Write a number sentence to help you solve each problem.

4. Ben measures the length of a leaf and a plant. The leaf is 15 centimeters. The plant is 57 centimeters. How much shorter is the leaf than the plant?

____

______ cm shorter

5. The picture is a square. Each side is 7 inches long. What is the distance around?

____

Distance around: ______ in.

Algebra Complete the number sentence to solve.

6. What is the length of the rectangle's short side?

20 + _____ + 20 + _____ = 60

The short side is _____ centimeters.

Problem Solving

MATHEMATICAL PRACTICES

Solve the problems below.

7. Ashley's sunflower is 70 inches tall. Kwame's sunflower is 60 inches tall. How much taller is Ashley's sunflower than Kwame's sunflower? Write a number sentence to solve.

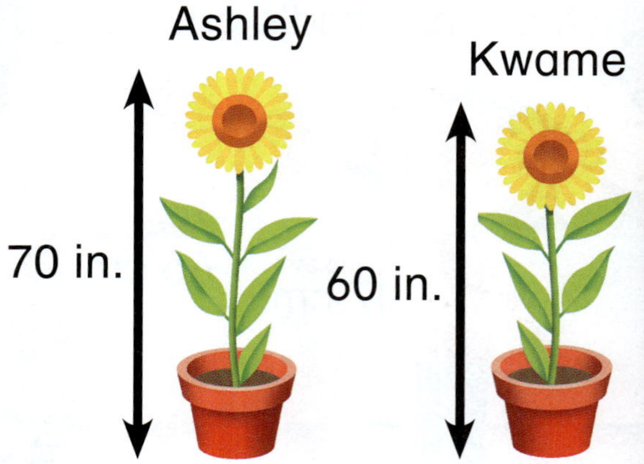

____

Ashely's sunflower is _____ inches taller.

8. What is the distance around the placemat?

28 in. Ⓐ

46 in. Ⓑ

56 in. Ⓒ

66 in. Ⓓ

9. **Journal** Draw a rectangle. Measure the length of each side to the nearest centimeter or to the nearest inch. Find the distance around the rectangle. Write a number sentence to show your work.

____

____

DIGITAL eTools www.pearsonsuccessnet.com

Name ________________________________

Lesson 13-6C

Comparing Lengths

1. Choose two paths: Their colors are _____ and _____.

2. Path: _____ _____ + _____ = _____

About _____ centimeters.

3. Path: _____ _____ + _____ = _____.

About _____ centimeters.

4. The _____ path is longer.

2.MD.4 Measure to determine how much longer one object is than another, expressing the length difference in terms of a standard length unit.

Home Connection Your child measured to compare the lengths of two paths.
Home Activity Draw a path that is made up of two parts. Have your child use a centimeter ruler to measure each part.

Which path is longer?
How much longer?

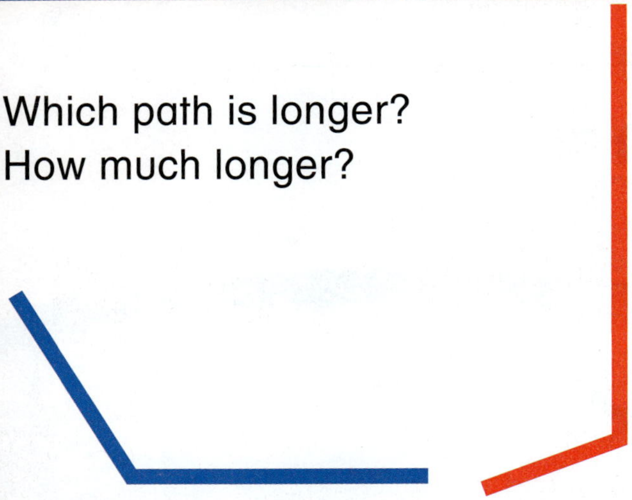

One part is about 3 cm. The other part is about 4 cm. Add 3 + 4 to find the length.

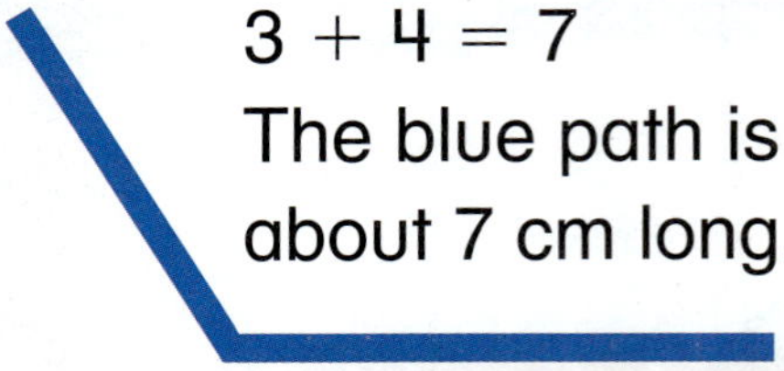

3 + 4 = 7
The blue path is about 7 cm long.

Guided Practice

Use a centimeter ruler to measure each path.
Then answer the questions.

Path A

Path B

1. About 10 centimeters

2. About _____ centimeters

3. Which path is longer? _____

4. How much longer?

_____ centimeters longer

Do you understand? Why can't you measure from one end of a path to the other to find the length?

One part is about 2 cm. The other part is about 6 cm.

$6 + 2 = 8$

The red path is about 8 cm long.

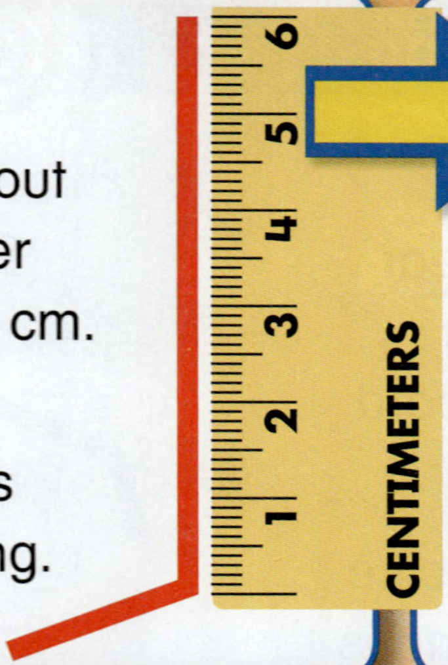

8 − 7 = 1.
The red path is 1 cm longer than the blue path.

You can subtract to compare lengths. The blue path is about 7 cm long. The red path is about 1 cm longer.

Independent Practice

Use a centimeter ruler to measure each path. Then answer the questions.

Path C

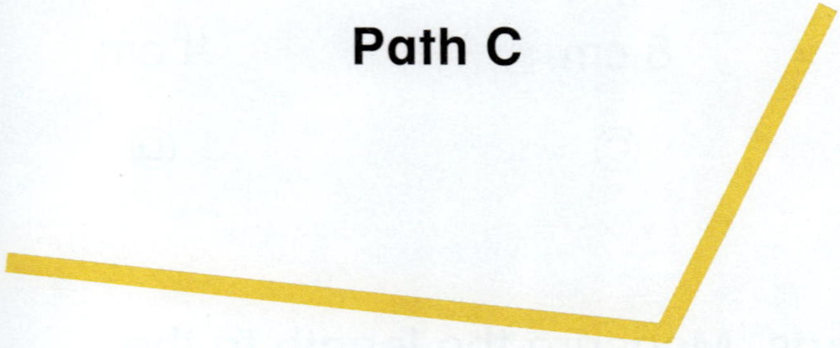

Path D

5. About _____ centimeters

6. About _____ centimeters

7. Which path is shorter? _____

8. How much shorter?

_____ centimeters shorter

Reasonableness

9. A key is about how long?

about 1 cm   about 6 cm   about 20 cm

Problem Solving

MATHEMATICAL PRACTICES

Solve the problems below.

10. Beth drew a model of a bike path near her home. Use a ruler. Measure the lengths of the parts of the path. Record the total length. _____ centimeters

Bike Path

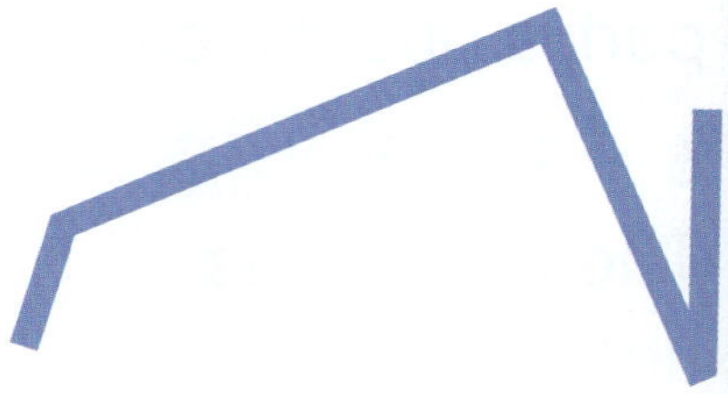

Ken, Beth's friend, drew a different bike path that is 6 cm long. Which drawing is longer, Beth's or Ken's? _____

How much longer? _____ centimeters

11. A path has two parts. The total length of the path is 12 cm. If one part is 8 cm, how long is the other part?

20 cm	10 cm	8 cm	4 cm
Ⓐ	Ⓑ	Ⓒ	Ⓓ

12. Journal Draw a path with two parts. Measure the length to the nearest centimeter. Write a number sentence to show your work.

How long is your path?

about _____ centimeters

_____ + _____ = _____

DIGITAL eTools www.pearsonsuccessnet.com

Name ______________________________

Interactive Learning
Lesson 16-2A

Graphing Lengths

Object	Length in Inches

0 1 2 3 4 5 6 7 8

Number of Inches

1. Which object is the longest?

____

2. Which object is the shortest?

____

3. Does any object have a length of 5 inches?

____

2.MD.9 Generate measurement data by measuring lengths of several objects to the nearest whole unit, or by making repeated measurements of the same object. Show the measurements by making a line plot, where the horizontal scale is marked off in whole-number units.

Home Connection Your child used a line plot to represent measured data.
Home Activity Gather and measure three small groups of objects with a ruler. Create a line plot with your child similar to those in the lesson to represent and compare your measurements.

Use a table to record the measurement data.

Object	Length in Inches
Glue Bottle	4
String	7
Feather	6
Scissors	4

Guided Practice

Measure each object in inches. Record each length in the table. Show each length on the line plot.

1. The marker is 4 inches long.

2. The crayon is _____ inches long.

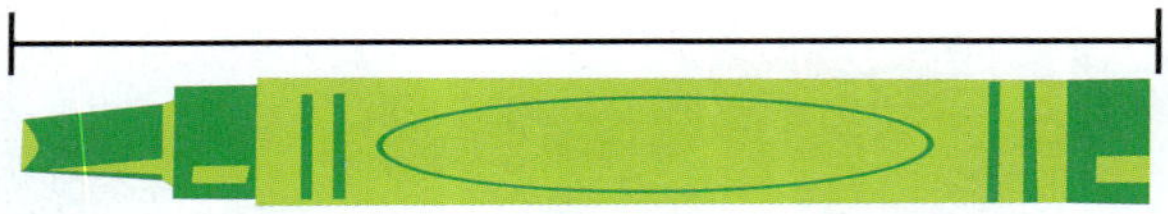

3. The paintbrush is _____ inches long.

Object	Length in Inches
Marker	4
Crayon	
Paintbrush	

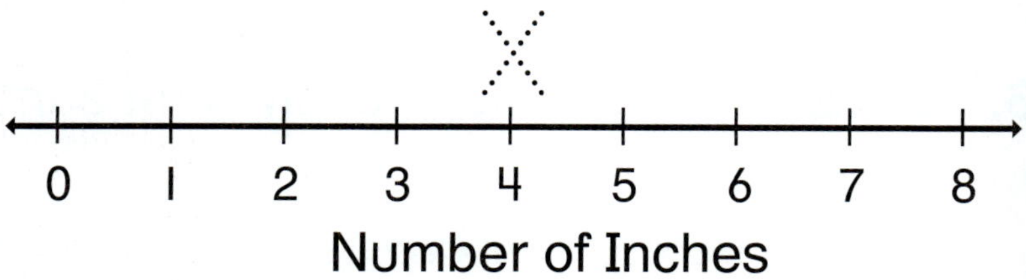

Do you understand? Which is the shortest object on your line plot? Explain.

You can use the line plot to show data you have collected.

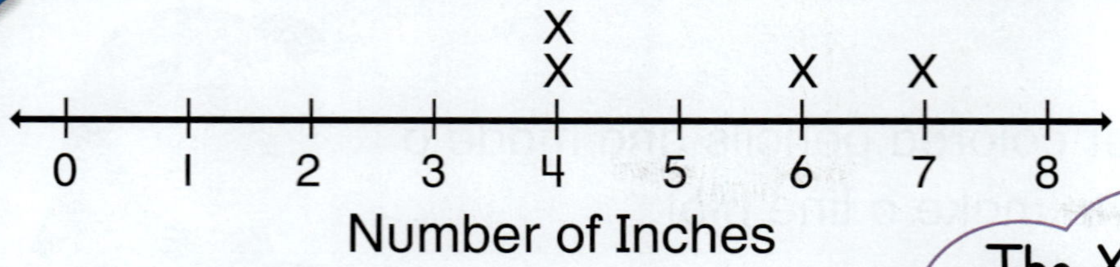

Independent Practice

Word Bank
line plot

Measure each object in inches. Record each length in the table. Show each length on the line plot.

4. The chalk is ____ inches long.

5. The straw is ____ inches long.

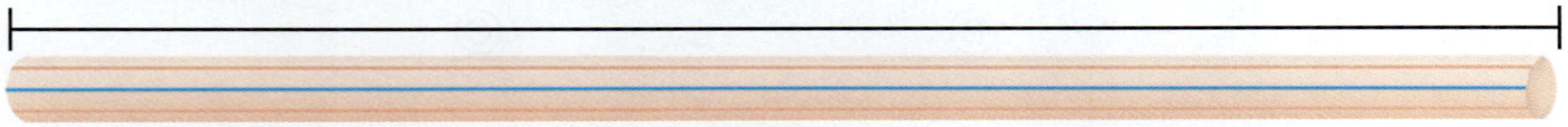

6. The craft stick is ____ inches long.

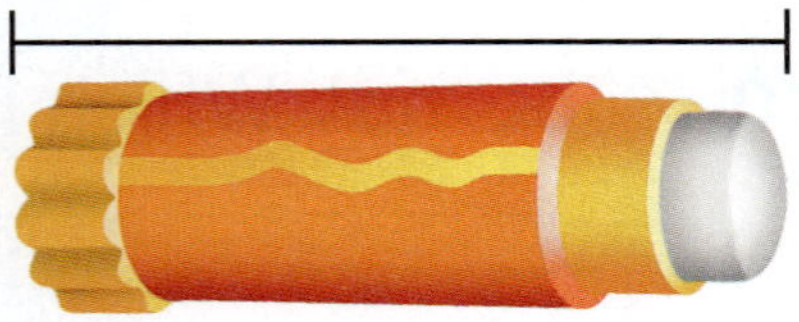

Object	Length in Inches
Chalk	
Straw	
Craft Stick	

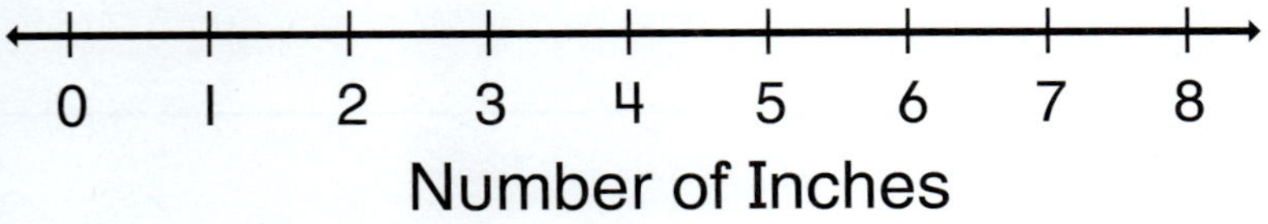

Reasoning

7. Write the objects from shortest to longest.

Problem Solving

Solve the problems below.

8. Sophia measured her colored pencils and made a chart. Use her chart to make a line plot.

Sophia's Pencils	
Color	Length in Inches
Red	4
Blue	3
Green	7
Yellow	9

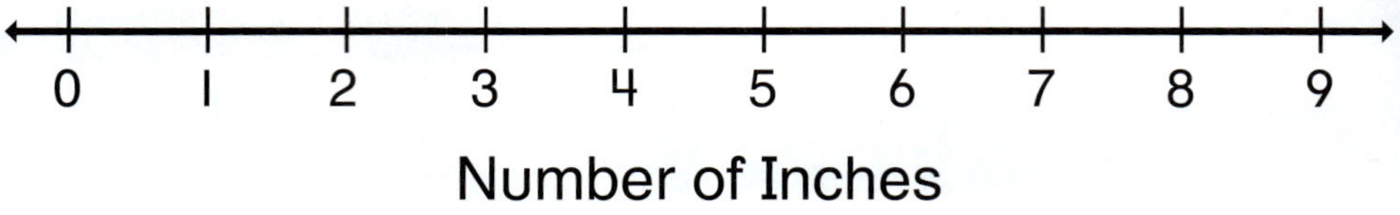

9. How many inches shorter is the red pencil than the yellow pencil?

Ⓐ	Ⓑ	Ⓒ	Ⓓ
6	4	5	3

10. Journal Which is Sophia's shortest pencil? Explain.

Name ______________________________

Interactive Learning
Lesson 17-6A

Skip Counting by 5, 10, 100 to 1,000

Skip count by:

1. **5s** What number comes next? _____

2. **10s** What number comes next? _____

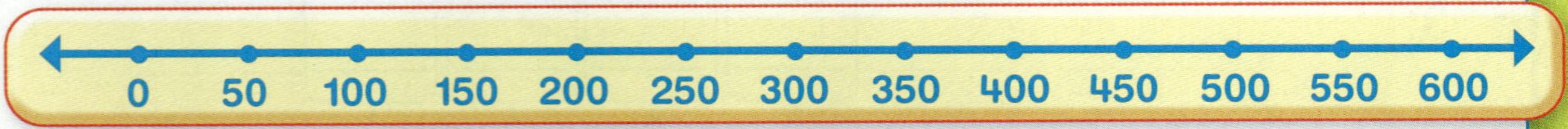

3. **100s** What number comes next? _____

2.NBT.2 Count within 1000; skip-count by 5s, 10s, and 100s.

Home Connection Your child skip counted by 5s, 10s, and 100s on a number line.
Home Activity Ask your child to tell you how to skip count by 10s on the number line and then identify which number comes after 20 in the pattern. Ask your child to explain how he or she knows.

You can use a number line to show skip counting.
You can start at any number.

This number line shows skip counting by 5s!

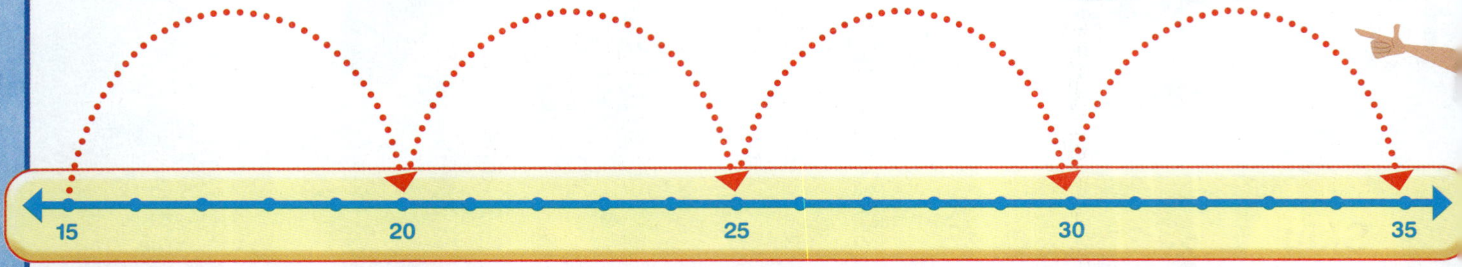

Guided Practice

Skip count on the number line.
Write the missing numbers.

1.

2.

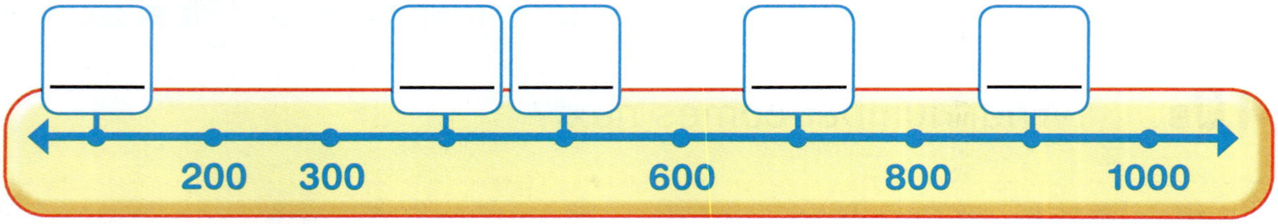

3.

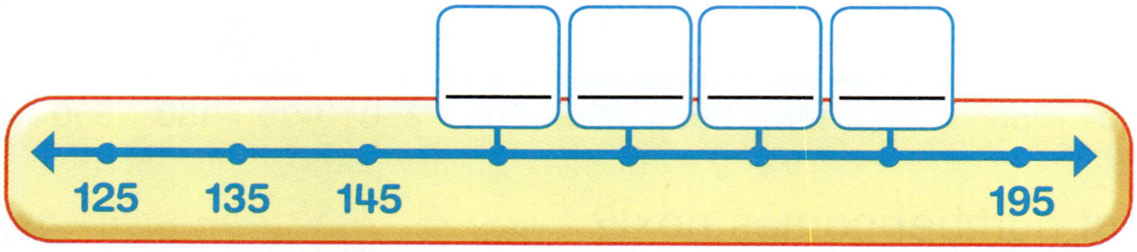

Do you understand? What number is used to skip count on this number line? How do you know?

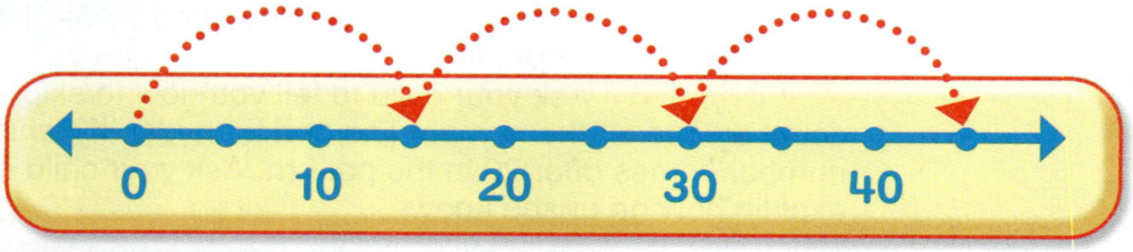

Skip count by 100s.

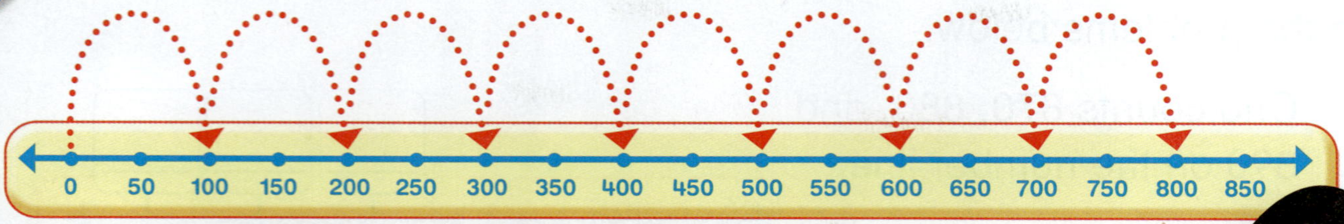

You can skip count even when you do not see all the numbers.

Independent Practice

Skip count on the number line.
Write the missing numbers.

4.

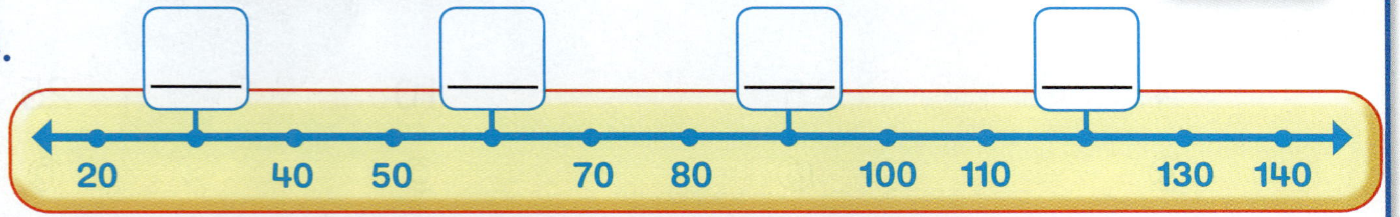

5.

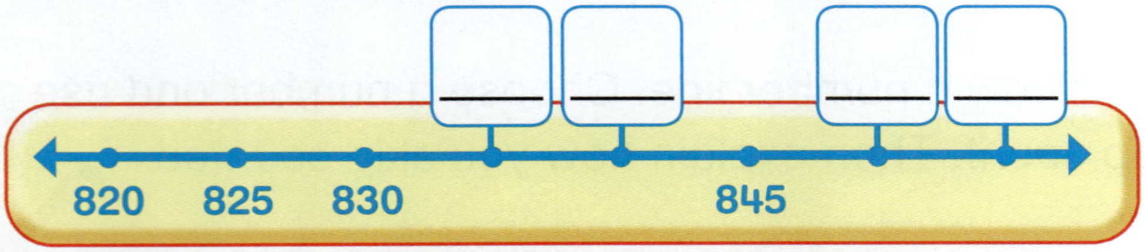

6.

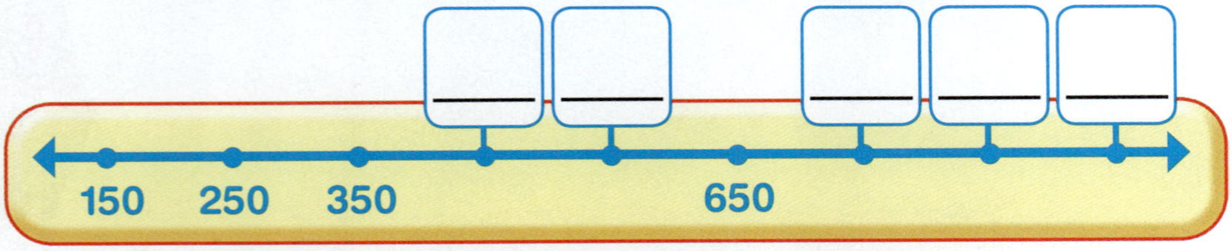

Number Sense Find the missing numbers.

7.

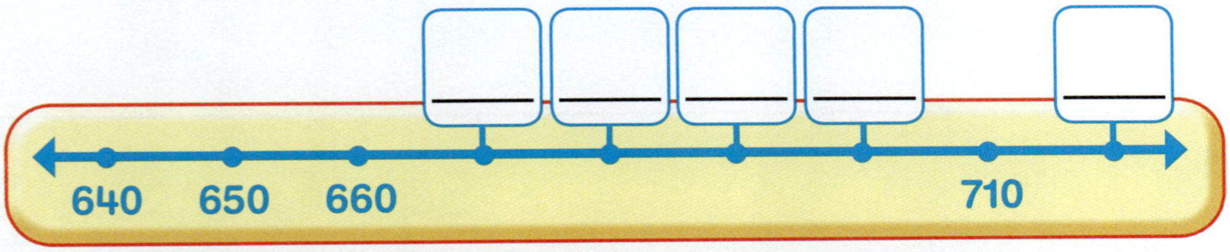

Problem Solving

MATHEMATICAL PRACTICES

Solve the problems below.

8. Cho counts 870, 880, and 890 on the number line.

What 3 numbers should she count next?

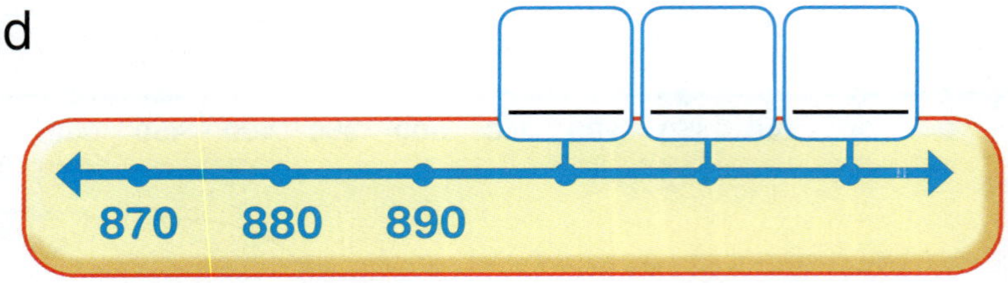

9. In his last four basketball games, Roy scored 10, 15, 20, and 25 points.

By what number do Roy's points skip count?

4	5	10	25
Ⓐ	Ⓑ	Ⓒ	Ⓓ

10. **Journal** Draw a number line. Choose a number and use it to skip count. Then explain how you skip counted.

Name ______________________________

Interactive Learning
Lesson 18-1A

Exploring Adding Three-Digit Numbers

1.

____ + ____ = ____

2.

____ + ____ = ____

2.NBT.7 Add and subtract within 1000, using concrete models or drawings and strategies... and/or the relationship between addition and subtraction; relate the strategy to a written method. Understand that in adding or subtracting three-digit numbers, one adds or subtracts hundreds and hundreds, tens and tens, ones and ones... Also **2.NBT.8, 2.NBT.9**

Home Connection Your child explored different ways to add 2 three-digit numbers with and without regrouping.
Home Activity Ask your child to show you how to add 305 + 497. Have your child explain every step of the addition.

Find 365 + 196.

One way to add is to add the hundreds, the tens, and the ones.

$$\begin{array}{r} 300 \\ +\ 100 \\ \hline 400 \end{array} \qquad \begin{array}{r} 60 \\ +\ 90 \\ \hline 150 \end{array} \qquad \begin{array}{r} 5 \\ +\ 6 \\ \hline 11 \end{array}$$

Then add the sums.

$400 + 150 + 11 =$ **561**

Guided Practice

Add any way you choose.
Use models if needed. Show your work.

1. $223 + 106$

$223 + 106 =$ 329

2. $149 + 362$

$149 + 362 =$ ____

3. $171 + 202$

$171 + 202 =$ ____

4. $421 + 397$

$421 + 397 =$ ____

Do you understand? Look at Exercise 4. Can you find another way to add 421 + 397?

Another way to add is to use easier numbers.

196 is 200 − 4.
So, I can add 200,
then take away 4.

365	565
+ 200	− 4
565	**561**

Both ways get
the same answer!

So, 365 + 196 = 561.

Independent Practice

Add any way you choose.
Use models if needed. Show your work.

5. 151 + 324

151 + 324 = ____

6. 250 + 298

250 + 298 = ____

7. 258 + 109

258 + 109 = ____

8. 187 + 246

187 + 246 = ____

Reasonableness

9. Jamal says that the sum of 183 + 178 is less than 300.
Is Jamal's answer reasonable? Why or why not?

Problem Solving

MATHEMATICAL PRACTICES

Solve the problems below any way you choose.
Use models if needed.

10. Maggie collected a lot of stickers for her album. She gave 129 stickers to her friend. Now she has 268 stickers left. How many stickers did Maggie have before she gave some away?

____ stickers

11. On Friday night, 156 people go to the school play. On Saturday night, 148 people go to the school play. How many people go to the play in all?

292	294	302	304
Ⓐ	Ⓑ	Ⓒ	Ⓓ

12. **Journal** Write an addition problem about stickers. Add 2 three-digit numbers. Solve the problem. Use pictures, numbers, or words.

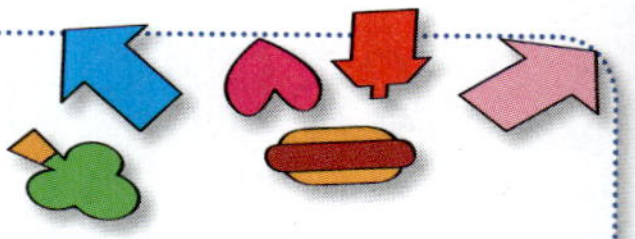

DIGITAL eTools www.pearsonsuccessnet.com

ame ______________________________

Lesson 18-5A

Exploring Subtracting Three-Digit Numbers

1.

___ − ___ = ___

2.

___ − ___ = ___

2.NBT.7 Add and subtract within 1000, using concrete models or drawings and strategies... and/or the relationship between addition and subtraction; relate the strategy to a written method. Understand that in adding or subtracting three-digit numbers, one adds or subtracts hundreds and hundreds, tens and tens, ones and ones...

Home Connection Your child explored different ways to subtract 2 three-digit numbers with and without regrouping.
Home Activity Ask your child to show you how to subtract 431 − 216. Have your child explain every step of the subtraction.

Find 372 − 123.

I'll count back to find the answer.

I'll try to think of numbers that are easier to work with to help me.

One way to subtract is to count back.

Start at 372. Count back 1 hundred, then 2 tens, then 3 ones.

100, 10, 10, 1, 1, 1

372, 272, 262, 252, 251, 250, 2

Guided Practice

Subtract any way you choose.
Use models if needed. Show your work.

1. 485 − 138

485 − 138 = 347

2. 342 − 154

342 − 154 = ____

3. 598 − 361

598 − 361 = ____

4. 321 − 115

321 − 115 = ____

Do you understand? Look at Exercise 4. Can you find another way to subtract 321 − 115?

Another way to subtract is to use easier numbers.

$$\begin{array}{r} 372 \\ -\ 122 \\ \hline 250 \end{array} \quad \rightarrow \quad \begin{array}{r} 250 \\ -\ \ \ 1 \\ \hline 249 \end{array}$$

So, 372 − 123 = 249.

Independent Practice

Subtract any way you choose.
Use models if needed. Show your work.

5. 794 − 452

794 − 452 = ____

6. 871 − 355

871 − 355 = ____

7. 649 − 574

649 − 574 = ____

8. 423 − 297

423 − 297 = ____

9. Reasonableness Leo says that the difference of 526 − 232 is greater than 200. Is Leo's answer reasonable? Why or why not?

Problem Solving

MATHEMATICAL PRACTICES

Solve the problems below any way you choose.
Use models if needed.

10. Tia and her friends collect cans to raise money for school. During the week, they collected 569 cans. On Saturday, they collected some more cans. Now they have 731 cans. How many cans did Tia and her friends collect on Saturday?

_____ cans

11. On Saturday, 214 girls and 186 boys played in soccer matches.
How many more girls than boys played in the matches?

28	38	128	138
Ⓐ	Ⓑ	Ⓒ	Ⓓ

12. **Journal** Write a subtraction problem about recycling.
Subtract 2 three-digit numbers. Solve the problem.
Use pictures, numbers, or words.

DIGITAL eTools www.pearsonsuccessnet.com